The Tenant's Guerilla Guide To Office Leasing

The Tenant's Guerilla Guide To Office Leasing

◆

For Tenants Large and Small

Control the leasing process and outwit the Landlord

Christopher Davis Desloge, Sr.

iUniverse, Inc.
New York Lincoln Shanghai

The Tenant's Guerilla Guide To Office Leasing
For Tenants Large and Small
Control the leasing process and outwit the Landlord

iUniverse, Inc.

For information address:
iUniverse, Inc.
2021 Pine Lake Road, Suite 100
Lincoln, NE 68512
www.iuniverse.com

ISBN: 0-595-31166-0

Printed in the United States of America

Contents

ACKNOWLEDGEMENTS

In grateful appreciation to my many friends in commercial real estate and to my many dedicated clients with whom we have shared some great memories to make business fun.

To such honorable people with whom I have had the privilege of working and whose integrity I surely admire, I thank Bob Kresko, Burt Follman, Tim Convy, George Convy, Gerard Mudd, Tom Kahn, John Pound and others, too many to mention ergo my fading memory. My landlord friends will hate this book, but their admiration and respect for me has fostered my confidence to write it.

I reserve my greatest admiration for my great wife Mary and my men Chris, Ray and William who have so earnestly stood by me throughout.

IN MEMORIAM

Writing this book provided me with the opportunity to give back to others what I have learned in real estate. In focusing on such a single-minded topic as office leasing and in attempting to finalize this book, I developed a form of tunnel vision on this topic, occasionally forgetting about the people that live in offices every day. My family lived in the New York area on September 11, 2001 and I watched as the south tower fell. The vivid images of men and women, jumping hand-in-hand from the buildings still haunts me. In fact, in my town we lost nine very sweet people, and many others were injured physically and emotionally. My friend Malcolm was in the World Trade Center in 1993 when bombed and again on 9/11. He survived only physically, and carries a great personal mental injury from which he, like so many others, may never fully recover. I think about the routineness we put into "going to the office" in an effort to better our lives, our wives and husbands and our children, and I think about how innocent people were taken from us that day, and of the thousands of heroes. When boarding a plane in Boston, no one expected to be killed flying into the twin towers of the World Trade Center that morning. Office leasing seems so trivial compared to such a catastrophe where our innocence was taken. I feel more of a patriot because of these strong emotions and for my more caring feelings for others. I remember our fallen countrymen and women. I remember the citizens of the many nations who died that day. I remember their parents, their families and their children. I honor their memory because in doing what was routine in their daily lives, going to the office, they gave us a new reason, a new definition to be proud. As we go to the office each day and kiss our little ones good bye, it is important to remember those that did the same and did not return. I doubt office leasing is noble, but people are noble. May the lives of those noble people never be forgotten, and may we each day see the righteousness in doing our daily work.

INTRODUCTION

Whether the climate for office leasing is oriented toward the landlord or the tenant, the "business protection" aspects of office leasing prevail as a priority. As you begin reading this book, I must first welcome you aboard for what will be an interesting and enjoyable journey through an element of business management that will touch every aspect of your company. Whether it is the large corporate office of a conglomerate, a regional sales office or a small private company office, there are few other opportunities in a company's life to evaluate itself in such an intimate fashion than when it evaluates the need and use of office space.

Economically, the costs associated with office leasing can be staggering. For example, a firm leasing 10,000 square feet may be dealing with $3,000,000 in rent over ten years, expense increases of $75,000 construction cost of $300,000, moving costs of $25,000, parking costs of $200,000, design layout and construction drawings of $40,000, just to mention a few.

Leasing office space once was an enjoyable, exciting task for growing companies with their sights set high, but with a good grip on their wallet. It was a time when the major considerations were the office dimensions and where to put the file cabinets; and rental rates were accepted as secondary to the utility of the office need.

Times have changed. Typically, a firm's office leasing cost now is the second largest administrative cost behind salaries, taxes and benefits. Rental cost alone, however, is only the first consideration in leasing, albeit the largest component. There are several other categories that carry a great deal of liability to an office user if not reviewed and resolved prior to any lease.

Tenants need to spend solid time determining the existing requirements by first taking careful inventory of persons, furniture, offices, and files. Forecasting is needed to highlight any areas that will be expanding or contracting and areas within the company that should or should not be adjacent.

Although many buildings may seem friendly enough, each one must be reviewed carefully to determine the compatibility with the tenant's needs and concerns. It is necessary to prepare a detailed list of the building's assets, liabilities, physical condition, construction, heating and air-conditioning, fire protection, floor plan size, and many other elements for you to compare each detail accurately.

Operating expense increases that are billed to the tenant during their lease show up with a big surprise if the cost was forgotten or unbudgeted. Complete details of how the owner intends to operate the building will verify any "hidden" costs down the road.

Remember also that the cash allowance that is made available for constructing or remodeling an office must be determined to be fair, accurate and appropriate to the requirement. Another loss of dollars if not pinned down.

It is not at all uncommon for the board of directors of companies to have input on this topic considering its considerable financial impact; as a total cost as well as the contingent liability it represents over many years.

As a result of the great many aspects of leasing coupled with the great amount of time necessary to manage them, and the large financial commitment, there is an absolute need for process and detail management; that is the premise of this book. Your ability to successfully manage the leasing process will hinge upon the team you select to handle the details, and the posture you take in leading your team and negotiations with landlords.

There are many fine, professional real estate brokerage firms with experience in office leasing and particularly tenant representation. The commercial real estate business has witnessed a bit of a metamorphosis toward serving the tenant. While ordinarily agents have brokered office leases acting as either an owner's agent or a dual agent, it has become more common for each office tenant to be represented by their own agent. During the glory days of the tenant's market when two years free rent was in vogue, the agent was more of a glorified delivery person, simply poring over which pic-nic basket to take. However, as the market turns more to the favor of the Landlord, tenants find out fast that every foot of ground in the negotiations is difficult. Likewise, tenants are fast coming to the conclusion that it is not just the rental amount that needs managing, but the whole process. From the first thought about your impending lease expiration to the delivery of the last desk in the new office, the whole multi-faceted process requires a unified management team. No longer can a tenant simply depend on an agent to "find" office space, have Fred figure out what kind of needs there are, have your brother-in-law look at the lease and have Matilda call the moving companies.

It is the whole process which needs managing and which requires a paradigm shift on behalf of the tenant to recognize the need for a new management program to deal with the new problems. It is a "Tenant-Controlling" paradigm.

I started the first Tenant Representation firm in St. Louis, Missouri during the height of the Tenant market where office space and leases were plentiful. During the months of setting up my business, several large building owners were beginning to hurt financially. Many buildings were not performing well and the banks were getting uncomfortable. The overall concessionary market was generally angering all involved on the owner's side. I still have not figured out whether it was a bad joke on me, but I accepted an invitation to be the keynote speaker at a meeting of the local chapter of the Building Owners and Managers Association on the topic of Tenant Representation. In my youthful enthusiasm to describe to this group of landlords how I viewed the need for tenant representation and its benefit to the tenants, I suspect some in the audience did not share my enthusiasm. Standing at the podium in front of a hundred or more local owners, managers, bankers and vendors, many of whom I believe felt tenant representation was to blame for the tenant market, the temperament of the room was highlighted when, from the back of the crowded room, a large, hard dinner role was hurled at me reminiscent of a Nolan Ryan fastball. I got out alive; many building owners ultimately did get hurt, but the new found need for an advocate for the tenant was permanently in place.

Advocacy for the tenant was the beginning point for what is now required by all business; to manage the office leasing element no differently than any other great liability. In a manner of speaking, the office space should be looked at as a partner in your Goals and Plans, a tool to help. Look at this from a long range planning point of view. Allow your facility to be an asset or partner to that plan, not just office space. And although office space is real estate per se, real estate only plays a role in the total picture—don't think otherwise.

There are many examples of how having the knowledge, and the ability to apply the knowledge has paid many dividends to the tenant. Following are a few examples:

A large tenant close to signing a lease was advised by my company that we suspected that the operating expenses of the building as quoted by the owner were too low and that they had not provided evidence of their accuracy. Quoting a lower operating expense amount means that the tenant pays for all dollars above that amount. We advised that the lease negotiations would cease if the owner failed to deliver evidence of the actual operating expenses. The owner delivered an annual history showing that the actual expenses were $2.00 per sq. ft. higher than stated, which meant that commencing at the first anniversary of the lease the tenant would get a bill for $2.00 per sq. ft. multiplied by their square footage. The tenant was 30,000 sq. ft. Over the lease term the mistake almost made would have been for over $100,000. But knowledge prevailed. It is illegal in most states to knowingly misquote "Rent", such as this example clearly showed was the case. Reminding the landlord of the legal ramifications of such misquoting is an easy solution to assure that the figures you get are real. Go one step further; add such language in the lease.

Another large corporate tenant was at the stage when the lease was ready to be signed. Every last item was thought to have been negotiated to eliminate any surprises. We found that one single word in an Exhibit was missing, but because of its omission, no one noticed. In the very lengthy Exhibit which summarized the particulars of who would build the improvements and who was responsible for what cost, the language had been crafted to include the individual items to be constructed as taken off of the construction plans and the general contractor's list. (It is unnecessary many times to get this specific in the lease, about the exact number of electrical outlets, the lineal footage of drywall and so forth, and I address this later in the book). When it came to summarizing the carpet, the language detailed the type, weight, pile and manufacturer of the carpet. A price was generated to purchase the specified carpet and that number was included in the amount the Landlord was to contribute for overall Tenant Improvements. We realized that the price of the carpet seemed a little low for this type of carpet and discovered that the cost for the carpet's installation had not been calculated. For the 55,000 sq. ft. tenant with almost 7,000 square yards of carpet, the cost was $28,000 which the landlord would have billed the tenant as a construction cost over run. This was to be a "turn-key" build-out, wherein the Landlord completely build's the space; it costs the tenant nothing and the tenant moves in (turns the key) when the construction is complete. In these situations, any changes after the agreement require documentation and the cost is charged to the tenant. The landlord squabbled, thinking that we were nickel and diming them up to the closing. I even remember using the example to make our point, asking if they intended to provide electricity to the outlets or just install the outlets. Unimpressed, but they were wrong and agreed to include the word "installed" in the lease, eliminating the prospect of the tenant receiving a $28,000 bill; an expensive, single missing word which would have likely ended in a dispute or even legal action had the omission not been caught. This example serves two purposes: 1) that well meaning people can make mistakes and unintended omissions, and 2) some landlords knowingly create misunderstandings to their financial benefit.

These types of circumstances occur whether leasing in a tenant oriented market or a landlord market, but the greater the landlord market, the greater the need for tenant advocacy. In recessionary times, as well as reasonable times, the misguided lease-costs can be the difference between profitability and damage assessment.

An underlying principle to successful office leasing in addition to process management is Negotiations to Win—keeping the negotiations in control: making the building owner clearly aware of what it will take to accommodate your needs. Even in more landlord oriented markets, don't be intimidated. Allow the objective truth of what your needs are to be the driving force. In some markets the rent will not be to your liking, but of the elements over which you can demonstrate domain, they will be managed.

To tie all of the details into a livable and readable document, it is imperative to have a lease which has been modified to your point of view. It is important that the lease contain tenant-oriented lease clauses rather than simply accepting what the boiler plate lease says. To recite an industry adage, it is by no means an understatement that boiler plate leases are prepared "of the landlord, by the landlord and for the landlord."

You will start with a bit of a painful introspective review of long term requirements coupled with prudent business judgment. Allow the process to unfold before you and it will allow you to dissect each physical detail of your need while understanding the philosophical or political influences within your company. Just "looking" for office space does not in itself solve problems; rather, the location must prove itself capable of withstanding the test you create for it. There are no surprises when the homework is complete.

And whether corporate exec, CEO or entrepreneur—this system is set up for easy digestion and planning. LEVERAGE, BEING INFORMED and HAVING CHOICES are your benchmarks—always have more information than the landlord—Knowledge is power. The following chapters have been prepared to deal with the psychology of the relationship between the landlord and the tenant and to provide an overall spirit on how to remain focused on the goals of successful lease management.

In this book, I have purposely not dealt with the micro details of the real estate market, financial analysis, construction management or lease clauses. There is plenty written on these details, and any web search can provide great results to educate you on these. Instead, I have focused on those areas where you, as a tenant, can control the process with any landlord and be the winner for your company and yourself. If I can give you anything from my years in office leasing and real estate, it is the gift of always having control, always winning financially and never being surprised. Happy reading.

1

HIRING THE PROFESSIONALS

There may be a temptation to go about leasing office space your self, mono e mono with owners, agents, property managers and developers. You most certainly can and the nature of this book is to allow you to do so. But remember this book is about leverage; created from information; prepared by objectivity to deliver opportunity. Going it alone is done frequently and more often by strong-willed managers. And for those that wish to do so, use the tactics in this book to improve your position along the way. But please learn from my experience that you can still maintain control when you have a team you control working as your foot soldiers. Mr. Big Ego attorney, negotiator extraordinaire rolled back on his heels in pride as he explained how he made the landlord squirm and got a great deal; explained how every lease clause was modified. My experience told me to keep my mouth shut as I discovered he had done a good job in the rent, but had to pay quite a bit in extra tenant finish costs; had accepted a ridiculously low operating expense stop and failed to negotiate a renewal and expansion option. Further, he had "penciled out" the floor plans with no architect or space planner. He must have spent over 80 solid hours monkeying with this and at his $250 per hour rate, cost himself tens of thousands of dollars which would have been better spent working with money making clients.

AGENT

The team of intelligent counsel will be your best weapon at every turn. The best composition should include a top shelf negotiator/real estate professional. This can be a veteran or young buck, but must have the core competence of solid negotiation skills and mastery of detail management. As I have developed tenant representation as a specialty, seek out a firm which either specializes in tenant representation or has a broker who predominantly represents office tenants in a larger full service brokerage company. Don't be fooled by the "full-service" come-on the large brokerages serve up. You don't need their property management skills, you need a person with a poker face. Interview several, set the criteria as I have outlined and select one. Your relationship should be reduced to writing in an agreement stating the exact services you demand and the fee structure. The fee ideally should be paid by the landlord wherein you lease space. Don't worry that this some how creates a conflict of interest. Cost of sales is something every building owner knows about, just be sure your agreement clearly states your agent's exclusive representation of your interests. Your insurance agent gets paid by Travelers, but you trust him thoroughly don't you? Alternatively, you pay the fee, but your negotiations should include having the landlord reimburse you. For those agents that do not ordinarily represent tenants, but have a solid working knowledge of office leasing, you may need to educate them as to the guerilla process this book preaches and make sure they're completely aware how leverage is created for the TENANT, not the landlord (as their experience may persuade).

Having an exclusive agreement with your agent will assure everyone that the fee to him or her will be static; the same from building to building (avoiding any self interest) and it will tell the landlord that you are serious enough about your possible move to have hired an agent. Agents get paid on deals they do; this is their only form of payment. The agreement must demand that any outside compensation to the agent, like a trip as an incentive, must be disclosed. In the tenant hay days, this was quite common for the building owner to entice the agent to "sell" his building. I believe it is best to kick all that kind of stuff out and focus solely on a simple fixed or fixed percentage fee. Your agreement and this process supersedes all of this worry. The agreement with your agent should be submitted to the landlord and agreed to, and attached to the lease as an Exhibit to protect the agent's fee. I address the real estate brokerage fee in more firm and glowing terms at the end of the Tenant Improvement Allowance Chapter. Permitting, or insisting that the agent issue a press release to the local news papers will garner both positive press for the agent, but will be noticed by a great many landlords. The landlords making contact with your team first is an excellent way to increase your options and take advantage of their overtures.

ARCHITECT

An architect must be on the team and one that has particular experience with office leasing, interiors construction and space planning. You do not need a "space designer" who works more in fabrics and textures; you need another clear-thinking, fleet-footed answer person. Some of the best architects for the job can be found under the nose of the building owners. Owners pay damn good money for these people to work for them and architects can be easily brought aboard your team by asking. Again, an agreement should be in place; you pay the architect (because you don't want the landlord to interfere) and require that his fee be reimbursed to you by the landlord.

Your architect should have working access to a general contractor very familiar with interiors construction. This is very important. You will need quick access to nearly accurate pricing of office space construction even before you start negotiating with the landlord and you will be having daily conversations about construction costs.

Most architects provide drawings, renderings, and elevations using computer aided design. For ease of changing, and taking off construction units, your architect should have this capability. If not, he's behind the times and you should look elsewhere. Frequently the landlord will provide your architect with their electronic files of the existing building conditions and construction drawings.

Furniture procurement, while through you, is well organized under the architect's venue. From the micro details of modular partition measurements and components, through color and texture selection to preparing bids and procurement, the architect is best equipped to assure total conformity to your time schedule and limited foul-ups during the procurement period. Your architect is also best suited for reconditioning your existing furniture for ther new space. Modular partitions can be repainted and re-covered, desks and chairs can be reconditioned. These cost saving ideas also need time management as these items will require being removed from your space for reconditioning months before your move.

The architect will have two other critical roles; overall construction management and vendor coordination. Whether you have hired the general contractor to build the improvements to the office space or the landlord has done so, the architect must be the watchdog overseeing all processes to assure timely work, proper completion and met deadlines. In particular, when the landlord has hired the general contractor, there is a natural inclination to "let" the landlord manage the construction. Yes, he will. His AIA contract with the contractor will give him that management position. In this manner, at every turn to make a decision on appropriateness and changes, the landlord will usually favor himself. Your architect must have "super authority" over the construction to manage the landlord's management over the general contractor. This allows your team to be in charge, to approve changes and assure complete control. This does not mean your architect has to sit on the floor during construction; it simply eliminates the exclusive management rights from the landlord or the general contractor and gives you the leverage where it usually dries up.

This same period calls for the management and coordination of not just the general contractor's trades and sub-contractors (which is the general contractor's responsibility), but also those vendors which are your responsibility, such as computer installer, telephone equipment and installation, corporate art and furniture.

This will become your most trusted and worked member of your team as each detail successfully executed will have first been approved by this person and will avoid immensely expensive and time consuming screw ups.

ATTORNEY

An attorney is a must. You will be facing a 40 page monster lease with hair all over it and it will absolutely need to be negotiated to be much more favorable to you. Ordinarily, this cost will be on your nickel without any landlord reimbursement. Interview a few hot real estate attorneys with office lease document experience and hire the one with the poker face who cares about tenants. They say attorneys are deal killers. For tenants, they aren't. Every dime you pay the attorney to convert the aggressive landlord oriented lease to the tenant's favor will pay you many times over in the future.

LIEUTENANTS

Your team should also include a few key lieutenants in your firm which can speak for you in your absence and that are deeply familiar with the inner workings of the office and your future plans.

Appoint a team leader other than you (you're the team owner). This person ideally should be the real estate professional. Not because that is my paradigm, but because all elements will need to be coordinated through a single, well rounded, experienced source. Establish an agreement or at least an understanding how meetings will be held, who will chair them and who has responsibilities for which specific element. Again, since you're the team owner, allow your team leader to set agendas, schedules and chair meetings. This allows you to maintain the Chairman of the Board perspective, ask critical questions and offer critical review.

The idea behind your team is information flowing in both directions. Remember to delegate and back it up with the authority for them to do their jobs. And if you think any of your team may not wholly comprehend the concepts of this information and their role in your leverage, hand them this book and tell them to read it.

Create a schedule that is agreeable to all of you to ensure the timely discharge of each function. A schedule can be created using a "critical path" which can be created by your architect. This schedule can also be shown to any member of your team, vendors, building and owners to allow every one to buy in and be added to the schedule. When time slips, you will see it, be able to hold those accountable, with or without approved excuses, and catch a future problem developing early enough to act accordingly.

AGENT	Lieutenants	Architect
Present Lease Review	Select/manage movers	Criteria and Needs Assessment
Employee Distribution Map	Move facilitation	Building Technical Data
Trends and Data	Vendor Selection	Tenant Imp Allow
Site Selection	Lease Alerts	Block Planning
Financial Analysis		Space Planning
Op. Exp. Breakdown		Const Cost Est.
Government Issues		Const. Proj. Mgmt
Lease Negotiations		Furniture Procurement
Lease Synopsis		Vendor Coordination
Critical Dates		

TIME SPAN

Depending on the size of your leasing need, your temperament and the detail required to manage the whole process, it can take from 5 months to a year and a half to finalize everything. Most managers I have dealt with fall in to two categories. They've done this before and are getting ulcers thinking about the upcoming task or they've never done it and don't have a clue how detailed and unpleasant the process can be. In both cases, the tenant hadn't really totally scheduled the task or had misunderstood the level of the work. This book is to inform the reader of the very real aspects of the office leasing process, sensitize the reader to the particular components, and empower the reader to manage the process whether short or long.

Let me put the process upside down to better understand. The construction of the space will take from as short as 30 days to as long as 60 to 90 days depending on the level of detail, special construction and working conditions. A construction permit usually takes 7 to 30 days for the building inspectors and fire marshals to okay. Preparations of the actual final construction drawings can be rushed for small jobs in 14 days but ordinarily take 30. The lease document has to be fully negotiated with the attorney, drafted and signed by both parties and can take 30 days. The negotiations themselves can be protracted or abbreviated: 15–45 days. And the big package of real estate market analysis, physical technical review, architectural/design work, governmental issues investigation can 30–180 days. The beginning steps of determining Criteria, Needs Assessment and Programming can run 7–30 days and pulling together your team can take a half a month. As in any process, you can rush through and forgo anything other than signing the lease the landlord hands you. Alternatively, you might find a space ready to move in in 2 weeks. Start early. If you are a large tenant, start two years ahead. Develop your team, hire the agent. Time is ordinarily your ally in this process. Time opens other opportunities in landlord's markets and time doesn't allow the landlord or potential landlords the leverage they so often use to their advantage.

2

THE RENEW CONUNDRUM

Every tenant in the world has one thing in common: They already have a landlord. You may be considering the "lease project" because you have an actual need or desire to be elsewhere, or you may be dealing with this just because your lease is due to expire. The course of least resistance is easy ceratinly: just renew and hope for some good terms. Whether you are interested in moving or interested in remaining, do not use the term "renew" in your new vocabulary when speaking of your present lease. Yes, you have provisions in your current lease which speak about what terms might develop if the lease is renewed, but if you do go through this objective lease project, hiring your team, developing your criteria, needs assessment, real estate market analysis, building technical data information, discussing economic development opportunities, negotiating new rents and lease terms, how can you consider that you might remain at your present location as a simple renewal. I advocate that your present building and office area are just another of the several possibilities that you may end up in. Let's look at this from the landlord's point of view. If you leave their building, the landlord will be required 1) to immediately forgo rental income from your space during its re-leasing and re-construction period, 2) to lay out large construction dollars to modify the premises for another tenant, and 3) to make whatever concessions may be necessary to secure another tenant, such as free rent, moving allowances, etc. If you are a larger tenant, the landlord may be facing the expense of dividing your space to accommodate several tenants if there is no other tenant in the market exactly your size.

I call this the "burden". Think of this as a pot of money sitting right next to the landlord's desk that he will likely have to shell out if you leave. That is his nut no matter what. So, why should you not benefit from these dollars? To turn this around, many a tenant has gone out in the market and received excellent opportunities from many different landlords, and because of inertia or simplicity, the tenant just stayed put. It will take the same effort and time to remain as it will have to lease elsewhere (except of the move itself).

Consider your renewal option terms as just the first of many lease alternatives or, better, the safety net in the event of a catastrophic breakdown in your leasing efforts. If the landlord thinks you're leaving, he very much knows how big the burden is to him. He is expecting the renewal option's terms to be the framework. He is hoping they will be in play and does not have to recapitalize your premises for another tenant. Avoid having "renewal" discussion with the landlord. Don't call it renewal. Call it "Building Option One" to compare it to all other buildings you will evaluate. In essence your building is providing you with *two* opportunities: the one your renewal option declares, and the one you successfully negotiate using the open market as your backdrop of comparables.

The building owner will rarely get it. But the fact is you are considering leasing space in his building, AGAIN, not simply renewing. In this manner, all elements should be on the table for discussion, including tenant improvement allowance, concessions, etc. This takes a strong will on your part, but simply treat your current building as if it were one of the several others you are considering. And, if it is really in your heart to remain at your present location and negotiate the best possible terms, then having the objective information from the other buildings provides the justification to remain.

The real estate brokerage fee must also be included. Your current building always gets the last bite of the apple. You may have negotiated with several other buildings, but as soon as your current landlord understands this, his best financial proposal usually magically appears, and one you strongly will consider. Has the real estate agent performed his duty? You bet. Don't let the landlord tell you that the man or woman on your team for the last year that brought you to the point where the current landlord makes his best offer is not worthy of the full fee. I believe in the trial close. On any matter important enough to fight for, make sure you always have plenty of options and if one of the options fights back, tell them they are disqualified. Telling a building owner, developer or agent that they are disqualified, begets an apoplectic response. There are banks to answer to, there are investors to answer to, there are spouses to answer to. While their ego will suffer a little, advising what terms would reinstate their building in the "qualified" category will usually get it done. And unless there is an overwhelming measurable and damaging reason not to do so, tell the landlord to get lost. I speak of this again at the end of the Tenant Improvement Allowance chapter.

3

CRITERIA, NEEDS ASSESSMENT AND TENANT PROGRAMMING

If there is one aspect of the office leasing process that is usually over-looked, it is the lowly preparatory work to determine the exact requirements in play for office space needs. I have a greater appreciation for my painter who spent at least 40% of his total time at my home, scrapping and preparing the surfaces before carefully applying several coats of paint. I could have taken the bid I received from the back-of-the-truck college kid I really liked, but the work accomplished in the preparatory stages which allow for many years of maintenance-free enjoyment were impressive, even to this weekend painter.

Frequently, when office users are considering the office leasing issue, it is likely more a result of an impending lease expiration than any overarching need to make an adjustment in their space. Inertia is quite comfortable and I believe that if lease expirations weren't as frequent, there would be a great deal less consternation on the intimate details within the space, good or bad. In Europe, some firms have occupied the same space in the same building in the same town for decades and even centuries. Even firms with the highest of high tech fit right in on the forth floor of a four hundred year old building with no elevator.

Opportunity is in how you look at things. Lease expirations must be looked at as an opportunity to reevaluate your use of space, which starts with how your company operates functionally and determining the ideal.

Human nature frequently forces us to jump right into things we should be better prepared for. When you have decided that you want to start the process, it will be natural to want to go out and see some buildings, kick some tires, act like customer. Don't. I caution that in touring buildings, there is a risk of commencing the landlord's engines revving. This will generate many questions which are unanswerable and possibly actually start some form of negotiations that were unintended. This puts the cart way before the horse, and forces you to lose control. My suggestion is that you leave the urge to see buildings until you are in the best position to manage the information. This information flows from the needs assessment and criteria.

Establishing an exact summary of what is ideal for your company will establish a benchmark against which to test not only every other office space you may see in the upcoming year, but also your present space. Functionally, this is very pragmatic. In order to make the office leasing process as smooth as possible, establishing this definitive criteria allows you to test each building you may consider against objective criteria. Such subjective elements like view, image and feel can wait and be tested later, AFTER the objective test is met. Having this fixed test abbreviates the process of touring buildings as certain ones can be disqualified (or put on the runner-up list). Applying this test through your Leasing Team means that you avoid repeating your need over and over to multiple building owners and not telling any two the same information.

Whether a corporate executive, CEO or entrepreneur, this system is set up for easy development and planning. No single element during the leasing process will have such a profound impact on every other decision you make in the future other than the Criteria, Needs Assessment and Programming.

Needs Assessment are the physical, tangible items of your lease which measure how you use the space best to accomplish your business planning goals. Examples would include each individual in the office, each function from offices to storage, work areas, private offices and or modular partitioning, files, conference areas, kitchen or coffee facilities, break or smoking rooms, floor size, life safety requirements, parking, telecommunications, automation, supplies, board room, reception area, mail/copy room, executive dining room, storage, computer room, special electrical equipment, special HVAC requirements, law library, and floor weight capacity concerns.

The Criteria are the general senses that you wish to apply to the company such as image, client or customer perception, view from office, view toward or of the building from outside, distance from employee's or executive's homes, proximity to customers or vendors, corporate identity, other tenants in the building and services such as restaurants, service stations, banks, cash machines, and parking. You should address any political influences such as the owner or company head likes triangle offices, requires proximity to his/her country club or can only be in single-story buildings. Are there any real ancillary aspects such as, needing to be in proximity to biggest client (but you don't want him to know it), concerns about your competition, corporate identity as hindrance or help?

Programming is the interrelation between the Needs Assessment/Criteria and any property which may be considered. The programming also involves diagramming the tenant's functions to their preferred configuration, such as department growth, optimum adjacency and interaction (or need not to) with other company functions.

While some tenants and architects become enthusiastic about a building's image and "already design" prior to first determining the "does it work" elements fostered by the programming, these are the nuts and bolts only after which can the esoteric, design or architectural features be applied.

The architect on your team is best equipped to initiate these matters as he or she will be responsible for determining each location's compatibility with your chosen requirements, performing initial space plans to determine the preliminary layout of the space. The architect should also develop a "Bubble diagram" for quick future reference when attempting to qualify certain spaces or buildings.

Some deal of contemplation on the part of the team leader is required to plan forward in time what the needs of each department, person or function of the company will be three, five, seven or ten years from now. Not easy, but considering your business plan or general expectations, you should be able to make some best effort estimates. In addition to being important for just square footage at the outset of the lease, the results have a direct impact on your negotiations for expansion space, contraction rights, early termination privileges and Tenant Finish Allowances provided by the building owner.

After the programming has been roughed out with the appropriate square footage for each person, office, etc., the total square footage should be embellished to account for the common areas, corridors and general traffic areas. The total square footage of the net usable areas does not account for these common traffic areas within an office. As a general rule of thumb, the net square footage should be increased by around 20 to 25 percent, but the architect will be able to accurately determine these square footage based on your type of use; such as law firm or telemarketing.

MAPPING

It will be important to establish a map for purposes of memorializing several key elements in your evaluation. This map will include the estimated location of every employee in the company, key competitors, key clients and all candidate and finalist office buildings. In the old days, a large paper map with push-pins would work, but never was easily reproducible. Today, there are many cartographic, and street maps of very inexpensive software which print in full color that can be purchased at most office supply and software stores as well as on-line purchase locations on the Internet. Most office computer systems operate with Microsoft Office. A great map system compatible with Word, and Excel is Microsoft's Mapoint and is easily emailable.

The map is a great tool to graphically understand the geographical impact to employees who may be facing a longer drive time, to show the top brass the distance from their homes, to strategically address competitors. It becomes a good tool after the deal is done to explain visually the location of the new office in consideration of these elements.

In representing a major discount stock brokerage firm, we mapped the locations of every other competitor and concentration of largest clients. It became abundantly obvious that only one location would cut into the competitor's market area and dramatically increase our client's visual corporate exposure. We leased a space which actually overlooked the competitor and arranged to have large corporate identity put on the face of the building. The building fast became known by the name of our client and figuratively and literally overshadowed the competition. The map was the key representation to selling that location to everyone from the facilities person to the Chairman of the Board.

In creating an evaluation of your present office lease, be informed as to the special conditions contained within your present lease such as lease expiration, renewal options, and expansion or contraction options. The terms of these may be valuable in improving your leverage during the lease negotiations.

And while on the topic of your present lease, be reminded not to fall victim of a time-tested human nature mistake of treating your present Landlord any less objectively than any other landlord. Years of occupancy can lead to a friendly nature between a landlord and tenant, and just such friendship usually puts a crimp on the tenant's ability to play hard ball, or at least have some strength in negotiations. Landlords love tenants who are less than eager to confront them on lease negotiation issues. Your present office lease and building must be compared against the test you have developed. This is your company's future we are talking about; profit and loss, not a tea party. So gently inform them of your team and the criteria.

Upon the completion of the Tenant Programming, you may continue to have unanswered questions. This is natural and those outstanding concerns are important reminders to stay on top of the process as it is translated into negotiations and floor plans. Now you have the weapon to answer almost every question about your physical requirements. Without having to regurgitate your needs each time you speak with a building owner, broker or interior design firm, the completed Tenant Programming can speak definitively for you. This is the test you have set out to have all properties meet.

This is the first step in Gap analysis and while the process may be difficult or painstaking to fulfill, the result will be the single most influential tool for your understanding of the present to then intelligently layout a plan for the future. Now you fill in the gap.

4

THE MARKET

In most cases, the available office spaces and buildings are easily catalogued by the real estate professionals. They maintain inventory of listings from broker to broker, and some cities enjoy the availability of a single clearinghouse of this information. So it is reasonable to say that your access to office space and buildings will not be limited from one real estate professional to another. However, be sure to ask specifically how he or she does maintain a monitor of these to assure yourself that as spaces come on the market from time to time, especially if your lease project will take some time, you will have immediate access to such information.

A second, less mined source of lease availability information is the knowledge of existing office lease expirations. A good real estate professional will have at his or her finger tips the exact date of lease expirations around the area. It is after all their job to market to office tenants for representation, so mining this information is natural. In addition to the list of "available" or "listed" spaces, a good list of tenants whose lease expirations fall within your schedule will provide you with a hidden outlet for alternatives. These spaces rarely come on the market because the landlords of these buildings also are attempting to keep their tenant and renew them. Think about yourself for a minute. You occupy a nice chunk of space; you know when your own lease expiration is. How many tenants on the market which might be compatible with your space know about it? Knowledge of these provides you with a second tier of possibilities. Contact with the tenant of these potential lease expirations can give you secret indication of their intentions and whether approaching the landlord is viable. This is a better technique than contacting the landlord of these tenants because in so doing you reveal to the landlord that he has an automatic two players for the same space. But once you determine that certain lease expirations will likely result in a new vacancy not known to the market, this gives you the added weight with the landlord of being the potential automatic follow up tenant without having to put the space on the market and suffer the cost of the lease up period. And for your agent, his or her real estate commission will remain unchanged because you will a require that your agent's fee be apart of the transaction or no deal. The landlord can barely say no when the alternative is such a burden.

The tour, the tout.

When touring available spaces, you will be faced with everything from the never-occupied, new space to the dowdiest, chopped up, rat maze space. It is difficult at best to envision your future location in the very same spot now occupied by an out of business stock brokerage firm with hundreds of small partitioned offices. Likewise, it is fanciful to envision your new image in a space now resembling a cave, with no improvements, ceiling, HVAC, or walls; just gray, dusty, concrete floor as far as the eye can see. When touring these buildings, do not prejudge anything good or bad. It will be up to the architect to marry your needs assessment and criteria with each building (programming), and evaluate the existing conditions (and value) of improvements, and evaluate each building's technical data. The tour is to give you a general sense of the building, the image, the view to and from the building, location, access, and how you might envision your company occupying space there. This sense and the process of programming, technical data and improvement allowance evaluation will provide you with some elements to determine if the building is "qualified" or is simply a "prospect". As each building clears certain evaluations they become "finalists".

When being toured by the enthusiastic leasing agent or building owner you will be faced with a fire hose of information. Building owners and listing agents are proud of their buildings and they energetically espouse all the specific benefits of each detail. You will hear the importance of the recessed sprinkler-head escutcheons, variable air volume HVAC, full height solid core hard wood doors, different ceiling heights, different ceiling grids, different ceiling pads, door hardware, window sill height, etc. I toured several large buildings with a client once and it was actually funny how in one building the agent showed unbridled enthusiasm about his building's thermostatically controlled HVAC zone areas. We must have stood there, five grown men and women in suits, for five minutes listening about vacuum driven HVAC boxes in the plenum. At another building, the seasoned building developer walked five feet into the space, waived his arm out as if to show us in and said, "How about that view? You need to be looking over this view for the next ten years." Rarely did he touch on specifications of the building. He was clear that there will be a time for that among the technical professionals, but today was for the sizzle. And by mentioning a ten year lease, actually started the negotiations right there. Do not commit to memory the floor weight capacities or one-inch mini blinds. Further, do not be put off or limited by the pre-existing improvements of the past tenant. It will be up to your professional team to determine the usability of any of that and as compared to the landlord's improvement allowance. And, if needed, in one week the rat maze can be cleared out to the shell to start over. Just enjoy the tours. Afterward, you can declare which building fits your criteria of image. Your team will determine which is compatible with your criteria and which then drops on to the qualified list.

During the tour, you will also be asked many questions about your plans, your office layout, lease expiration, detail after detail. Remember that if you have properly performed the needs assessment and criteria, your team leader and architect will be qualifying the building. It is unnecessary to reveal all of your information at the tour, there is time enough for that later. The best bet is to not talk about anything other than the building you are touring.

Using this "prospect", "qualified" and "finalist" framework throughout your process will give you the permission to tell a building owner or agent that their building has been "disqualified" if they do not meet the terms you set for them. Sometimes just a negotiation ploy to get a landlord to agree, but having the predetermined permission to disqualify a building is powerful stuff. It provides you with leverage to outline what terms or conditions would return the building to a "qualified" or "finalist" stage. If you want to see angina in action, just tell a building owner that has just said no to your request for three more months free rent or more construction dollars that their building has been disqualified. You will likely get a call back from their bank saying, "Well, that would be just fine."

The immovable ego

We represented a tenant at a building where the landlord stated that there was no way in the world he would agree to allow the tenant to have signage on the building. I indicated that I was concerned that such a simple matter as a sign might interfere with the landlord receiving over $1,000,000 in rent over the term and I wondered out loud whether his bank would have the same point of view, and that perhaps I'd ask them. The phone was slammed down in my ear after some curt words about me and the horse I rode in on, and five minutes later his colleague called me and said, "Don't call the bank...we'll do the deal" Your real estate broker's fee may also see this fate, where the landlord's ego says no. Be prepared to meet the immovable ego with your predetermined agreement with your self to disqualify the building. It is refreshing, and you maintain control.

Existing Tenants

To round out a clear understanding of the market, it is genuinely a good idea to get the input from existing tenants in the buildings you are touring. By simply retrieving a roster of the tenants in the building directory or a reverse directory on the internet, make contact with the lead person, manger or owner of a variety size and type companies to discuss all matters that are important to being a tenant. Introduce yourself as a potential tenant. People like to talk and you will learn a great deal about how the HVAC functions, the personality of the building manager, the negotiations they achieved; and just listening to them talk will usually garner information on topics you did not think to ask about. Make good notes from these conversations as some of this information you may likely take to the landlord as part of your negotiations. We once discovered from another tenant at a building we were considering that the building management had a reputation of hiring only the least reliable and indifferent janitorial services company as well was almost always behind in making simple repairs such as public lighting. We learned that snow removal even was inferior. The building once was owned by an excellent and wealthy developer who had sold it to an individual investor who was lackluster in his management and spending money. We made certain demands of the owner, to hire a professional janitorial service, to agree to certain specifications for management of the property and attempted to make sure all these were in the lease. Interestingly, the owner's arrogance said no. So, because the other tenant had revealed to us this reality, we were able to avoid finding out way too late about the management, and then being dejected as a good paying tenant receiving sub-par service with no recourse. "One thin dime, and invest some time." In another case, just such conversations revealed items that the landlord eagerly agreed to, which made for a pleasant and honest transaction without surprises. Don't be bashful in asking about what kind of deal the tenant negotiated or what kind of personality the landlord has for negotiations. Without asking bold questions, one rarely receives bold information. In exchange, offer to provide him or her with the results of your negotiations or information. If you lease there, you have made a good neighbor (especially if the landlord one day hits either of you with a surprisingly high expense increase).

Negotiations

No one likes to be told what to accept, even if it is a thing we would agree to. In negotiating for leases, telling the landlord how it's going to be will likely get a hostile and unsuccessful response, even if he would have ordinarily agreed to more. Indicating that the acceptance of certain terms, comfortable or uncomfortable to the landlord, would keep their building as a finalist in your leasing comparables can say the same thing and garner a happy acceptance of your request. All landlords simply want to know they are still in the game. A clearly worded document drafted by you that is titled "Offer" has the air that if the items therein are agreed to, then there is an acceptance by the landlord. The reality is, your offer can always change later. If you know where you genuinely want to end up in all your categories, you needn't spill the beans up front, especially if it is reasonable to think that large dollar and term negotiations may be required to get to the end zone. Likewise, people never know when the negotiations are over. There are no yard lines painted on the floor of the conference room indicating that you are on the 10 yard line when you are negotiating a certain element of your lease. Sitting there with the landlord, they usually have no clue what terms you have left to negotiate. Like the old television show Columbo, the affable, bumbling police detective made persistent headway when, as his foil thought the questioning was over and he was heading out the door, he would stop and say, "Just one more thing...." In a lease negotiation, this can be successfully performed as you negotiate from item to item. If there are several very important elements that you must have agreement to and these may be bitter pills for the landlord to swallow, get the landlord pregnant with the prospect that in his mind many of the elements have been concluded. But he has no idea of the list of "just one more thing" items on your list. Good landlords routinely ask trial close questions to avoid such a trap, such as "Exactly how many items do you have that are important to you if I agree to this item?" Good stuff. Or, "I will agree to this item if you agree to conclude your negotiations." Another seemingly fatal blow. Not so. Always tell the landlord that these negotiations are in a comparative dynamic, that is to say that other buildings and your current building all are the measurement of whether the landlord's terms are agreeable. Remove the decision from you personally, or your company, and drop the monkey on the back of the market that you are evaluating. You may or may not have concluded that his building is the perfect spot and you are just trying to better the negotiations, but he should be unable to see that point if "the market" is still in play. Saying yes to a landlord, that you agree to his trial close does not prevent you from saying, "just one more thing…." at a later date.

Financial Analysis

You will receive every imaginable proposal to lease office space. It may come in the simple form of very little analysis required because the rent is a fixed amount for every month, and there are zero concessions to value, to the complicated form of being required to understand the real value of variable rental amounts, substantial free rent, cash for moving, assumption of an existing lease, planned increases in expenses, among many other components. In any event, it is best to have a mechanism capable of bringing any and all of the varying alternatives you will face back to a common and comparable financial base.

By using a software-based lease analysis program, you will be able to see your different leases side-by-side based on the total dollar amounts or net present value of the dollars over time; this system will also view your dollars of NPV relative to the "usable" and "rentable" square footage so you can see a pure and accurate financial comparison. You can develop several views of all the buildings considering planned or possible expansions and contractions in square footage. There are many affordable Lease Analysis software packages available on the internet. Look for the systems which are designed primarily for the tenant. These can be ordered to arrive by mail, but many now have download-able programs so you can start immediately. These systems let you change views and deal structures in a heartbeat, providing graphs and charts as well to visualize the dollars. These also help in making your presentation to colleagues and other interested parties to your lease.

NO is just the beginning of YES

Think for a minute about when the listing agent for a building you are considering supplies your team with the answer "no" to your inquiry for more tenant improvement dollars. Who is saying NO? And what degree of weight is to be put on the NO. Listing agents frequently have been given parameters of acceptable terms by their landlord client. Listing agents respond to Requests for Proposals every day. Listing agents have egos also and occasionally flex their authority. Listing agents have brokers. Brokers have landlord clients. The landlord itself may have numerous layers, the portfolio management team in one city, the property management team in another city, the legal team in yet another city and the equity holder in another. Each of these positions job is to say no. There should be a sign on their door saying just this, and it should be printed on their business cards. None of these positions gleefully throws caution to the wind and gives away freebies with seeming reckless abandon. But every day, these same people agree to leases all over the world with the same concessionary results because the crafty tenant negotiator understood this family tree of who will likely be in the decision stream. Local landlords also have a variable decision stream: the listing agent, the property management company, the owner, the owner's spouse, the owner's bank, the owner's attorney, and the owner's accountant. In one deal we did, the landlord's crazy brother-in-law who owned 5% of the building had input. Before you agree to accept their no answer, consider who behind them could agree. Just like you not wanting to spill all your jelly beans in your first step in the lobby, the landlord has his own negotiation tree to consider, usually giving only inches in the opening round. Frequently not even that. Understand that at every building there simply will be several rounds of negotiations, each one moving deeper into the financial give and take of the deal. Know where you are, what yard line you are on, how many other layers remain with the landlord to penetrate, don't get frustrated at many different "no" answers. Ultimately you will arrive at the point that no is either a yes, or it is an absolute no, but you never would have known that if you didn't push all the way past the one yard line.

5

PHYSICAL TECHNICAL DATA

Having dug into your own mind and operations during the Needs Assessment, Criteria and Programming stage, it will be time for the buildings in which you have preliminary interest, to *themselves* answer some questions about their compatibility to you.

From the street or inside, an office building usually seems generally acceptable, with no particular reason not to consider it. In fact, once a group of buildings has made your short list, it may be indeterminable as to the differences between them. Financially, you will be determining rent and other costs through the negotiations, but the physical elements are to be evaluated to support and to be used in conjunction with the financial analysis. Do not discount the importance of this research. It must be completed. There are critical structural aspects and life safety issues which need disclosure. More mundane things such as elevator speeds, ceiling height, electrical and telephone distribution and HVAC are as elemental to your decision as the look and price of the building.

This step is excellent in capturing all the non-financial differences building to building where some items are seen and in place, and others are omitted or missing.

By way of example, a company leased 30,000 sq. ft. for their corporate offices. Within the corporate offices was a considerable law library that, at first blush, seemed antiseptic enough. However, during the construction of the floor (of the new development) for this tenant, a sharp engineer raised the issue of the floor weight capacity as compared to the actual weight that would be incurred by the fully laden library. It was determined that in fact the library represented an average weight of over 140 pounds per square foot while the floor was designed to accommodate no greater than 100 pounds per sq. ft. This required extensive structural modifications to the floor, delayed construction to the space, delayed the lease commencement which caused the tenant to holdover at their old location for several months at double rent. In addition to charging the tenant for the cost overrun to bolster the floor structure, there were penalties for delayed occupancy at the new building as the modifications to the floor created a considerable delay in the overall construction of the office tower interfering with the timely commencement of several other tenants. Very unpleasant.

As you can see, the requirement of completing a Building Technical Data Form is no small matter. After the building has passed the preliminary muster of your architect, which is that the building meets your Criteria and Programming and you have an interest, most sophisticated commercial real estate architects use Technical Data Forms consisting of nearly every physical element of a building. Your architect should then report to your team what, if anything further, is required to further qualify the building. It is okay if there is something wrong, even something very expensive to modify, but that must be determined very early, injected into the lease negotiations (when the leverage is the highest) and develop a solution through your team and with the landlord. It is not cool to either have wasted time going down a path which may not work or, worse, discovering a major, technical, financial problem after the deal is struck.

It may be likely that you actually come to know more about the building than the owner.

An example of building differences that matter to you are sprinkler systems and life safety features. In an office building, that has several floors as well as the larger office towers, life safety controls are essential, in my opinion. Without the availability of an emergency generator to provide emergency lighting, emergency smoke removal in elevator shafts, stair cases and floors and emergency communication for fire fighters, a building's purported beauty, nice floor plan and view aren't worth the risks. No where are there more toxic smoke-emitting materials than in the synthetic materials found in office furniture and carpet.

Asbestos impregnated materials in older buildings are common. While that alone may not set off any alarms in you, try making modifications to your space or running wires in the ceiling plenum and the issue of carcinogen asbestos at your company will become its biggest problem.

Having represented an international insurance company in their leasing of over 40,000 square feet, among other criteria, they were mandated by their board of directors to NOT lease space in any buildings that do not have modern life safety features and that contain asbestos.

This will highlight different types of HVAC from building to building. Some are quite efficient while others are antiquated and obsolete. It is important for the building owner to provide reasonable assurances as to the cooling capacity and heat expected. You can find the greatest deal in town, but if the AC or heat is lacking when you move in it will be a worthless deal.

SPACE MEASUREMENT

A direct and large financial component in your evaluation is the exact formula the landlord uses at each building to measure the office space. The usable area is simply that area of the building within the confines of your demising walls and exterior; no fancy explanation. While there may be some differences about space occupied by a large group of pillars, deep air conditioning units at the window, vertical penetrations such as elevator shafts and duct, and without dwelling on the minutia of this, the usable space is that area which you will occupy and use.

Building owners got smart years ago when they leased whole floors to tenants who "used" the whole floor. Then when they had to break up floors for multi-tenants and add corridors, they added up the usable again of the remainder of the space and, low and behold, they had less usable area. The area to lease got smaller; the rent was the same so the landlord got less money. Not for long! For many years there were as many different measurement styles as there were landlords. To standardize, (there's that word again, but in this case its good) the Building Owners and Managers Association developed a set group of measurement criteria that ideally could be uniformly used on any building. This method is published by BOMA as the *American National Standard Method for Measuring Floor Area in Office Buildings.* Of course the rouge landlord may still measure to the corner drug store, but now the Tenant has ammunition too.

Your architect will immediately be able to determine the usable, no problem. With that in hand you need to determine what the "load factor" is in the building; that percentage increase to account for the proportionate share of common areas. Do not take the quoted load factor (known in some cases by its reverse calculation, "Effeciency") for gospel. Some landlords may use the wrong number or make one up to fit the market. Some agents will tell you to negotiate it. Well, without a yard stick or knowledge where it should be, you're just guessing. No guessing! Indicate to the landlord that you assume that the BOMA measurement applies in the building. Only a foolish landlord would answer no (or an uninformed one, but that's to your advantage). Then simply follow the example of the BOMA method to determine the REAL rentable. If your number is higher than the landlord's, shut up, if lower you have a bona fide case to dispute his accuracy. In this case, indicate that you are prepared to move forward with the building only if the measurement (which multiplied by your rate you have negotiated) is fixed by your calculation or that you may disqualify the building.

In some egregious cases, and I remember a few myself, the Landlord can add up all the "rentable" square footages on the lease documents in his building and actually arrive at a total square footage larger that the building itself.

The difference between rentable and usable is also referred to as the "rentable-to-usable ratio", which is important to consider when you are boiling all of this down on your financial analysis which will back-calculate what each building is actually costing you on a usable basis for net-net comparisons. Some buildings will seem cheaper at the rental rate than others at face value, but catching the measurement differences may add up to costing more in the end analysis.

AFTER HOURS AND EXCESS USE UTILITIES

CPA firms and attorneys in particular create an inordinate demand on HVAC as they may occupy space at night or on weekends. Firms that create a substantial demand, such as 24 hour operations, may be better served to have all utility service metered separately, thereby not having the owner as the bookkeeper. Some buildings have master systems that turn on the whole building when demand is called for anywhere in the building. Others have multiple separate systems which service portions of the building. Many owners make this direct charge a profit center charging astronomical hourly amounts while others charge the actual costs. But you need to know these things before the lease is signed.

The technical data form provides for the owner to indicate these times as well as the cost per hour for such service after hours. The owner may prefer that this be separately metered to prevent any charges seeping on to his responsibility which they may have to pass on to the tenants. As a warning to you, in addition to discovering what additional costs you may face, you do not want to be paying increases in operating expenses that the owner should have collected from other abusive tenants.

HVAC

The number of HVAC zones is critical and the management of your own comfort within your space depends greatly on the flexibility of the HVAC system. Some deliver varying volumes of air and or at varying temperatures to different areas of the office. Others deliver a constant volume of air at constant temperatures. Some buildings suffer miserably by the effect of solar radiation and require some additional AC tonnage to cool. The southern side of one building may be hotter as the sun beats down, thereby creating demand for less heat internally (or maybe air-conditioning to offset the solar heat) while the other side of the building will be normal temperature calling for only typical building-served air supply.

The perpetual conflict between forced air conditioning and perimeter baseboard heat also is a killer as people at the perimeter will get the most heat while those in the interior are provided with less; cold sometimes. These two systems have a history of competing also. That is, while the perimeter heat is heating, it sends signals to the air flow or air conditioning thermostats to cool down, which it does and tells the heat thermostats to provide more heat. A round robin that usually ends up with many calls to the building management to adjust the system. Talk to the tenants already in the building; this helps tremendously.

If the system has flaws, have them negotiated now. Make arrangements for the addition of more zones (at the landlord's expense, not from your Tenant Improvement allowance) or to follow the recommendation of the HVAC specialist. Then back it up with language in the lease which marries the landlord to making the building HVAC system perform up to his word, or else.

ENERGY MANAGEMENT SYSTEMS

Many buildings built in recent years have been built with computer Energy Management Systems that govern many of the building's operations. The cost of utilities has mandated greater cost control. Many years ago it would be indifferent whether the electricity was used for a couple extra days per month; the utility cost was so affordable that a couple of extra bucks by the owner went unnoticed. To the contrary today; the inability of a building owner to recoup excess costs could very well be the difference between profit and loss. Energy Management Systems can range from a sophisticated master system to the simplicity of a personal computer that runs all aspects of the building. Electricity can be shut off after hours, lighting can be cut, the security system can monitor who enters and leaves the building. The real benefit besides the control of these aspects is that the after hours utility costs and excess use aspects can be governed with ease and billed to the appropriate party as opposed to just having the building pay and then increase the operating expense pass throughs to all tenants. An energy management system is really a tool for the landlord to better manage and govern typically unmanageable issues. The tenant gets to borrow the benefit by having a better run building. For those buildings without these, and if the building operating costs start to get out of hand which generates bills to you for increased operating expenses, negotiate that the landlord must install this type of system to alleviate the abusive costs. Add language to the lease which forces the landlord to do so. Without the language, the landlord has little incentive to act at all. Just keep sending you bills.

FLOOR CONSTRUCTION

Buildings are constructed in a variety of ways depending on local custom, cost considerations and design. Mostly you will find only two: skip pan concrete and concrete poured on metal deck. Concrete floors that are several inches thick are excellent sound barriers and very solid allowing for virtually no concern for placements of heavy areas like file rooms and libraries. Metal deck types are ordinarily less dense, are accustomed to some noise transmission and may actually spring slightly with heavy traffic. If libraries or heavy file storage areas are too used, special care needs to be taken as to their placement within the space which may or may not impact the overall design of the space. If you may be leasing several floors together, an internal stairway may be a possibility to reduce wait time for elevators and increase ease of movement. Certain structural criteria will determine where or if this is a possibility, again another item for your architect.

DISTRIBUTION—ELECTRIC, TELEPHONE

Dull stuff, but a key question to being able to handle all of your electrical, data and telephone needs now and in the future. If not adequate, more may be required in the future. The landlord isn't going to pony up for that after your lease is signed, but if you believe it will be needed, have it upgraded as part of your negotiations now. It can cost tens of thousands of dollars to upgrade electrical distribution with transformers, buss ducts and panels, so be sure the pretty building at the good rent contains the services required to operate.

ELEVATORS—HOW MANY, WEIGHT CAPACITY, SPEED, PARKING, FREIGHT

Some buildings have beautiful elevators that whisk you to your floor at Captain Kirk speed. Others barely get to the floor, open two inches below the floor, are also used for freight or parking. Be sure to identify the value to you, positive or negative, of the elevators, their use, speed, safety, and weight capacity. A separate freight elevator is always a God-send to avoid sharing an elevator with an upright marble conference table or having to wait while one elevator is "out of service" being used for freight. Some high-rise building elevators are programmed to "station" themselves at mid points in the tower and wait for a call, making wait time shorter. Other elevators just sit where they last stopped, and may have to run 10 floors to get to the next call. Time is money and most buildings will have their elevator contractor provide a "wait time" report for you. If you have two or more floors in a building, wait time can cost you big money as your people stand around. Wait time can be calculated and added to the financial analysis.

LIFE/LIFE SAFETY, SPRINKLERS

There are many systems which help save lives now in office towers. And most contemporary fire districts and marshals apply these new standards to new buildings. Fear however the old grand building that lacks in total fire and life safety. Do not take anybody's word for anything with life safety. All building owners will firmly claim the approval of their life safety by the fire marshal. One building may have nothing more than pull stations and lighted fire exits and another will have smoke detection in the return air plenum and in the occupied areas, emergency lighting, automatic smoke removal systems, "positive pressure" stair cases and elevator hoist ways, emergency annunciation systems which automatically announces throughout the building specific emergency instructions, emergency firefighter telephone jacks, and all powered by an emergency power generator in the event of a power failure.

Sprinkler systems are very important, especially in mid and highrise buildings. The cost of installing one in a building that does not have any can be astronomical and will likely not be installed because of your leasing, unless you are huge. If installed, routine maintenance is performed. Be sure to negotiate that you be notified in advance of any sprinkler or fire protection repair anywhere in the building, not just in your space. You should be clearly aware when the building is not protected with sprinklers (because some part has to be ordered from Timbuktu) so that you can make other emergency plans if a fire does break out during an unprotected period.

Do not pass over this component lightly. Many of my clients who have occupied the older buildings when evaluating their renew vs. relocate ideas, almost always recognize their lives, their families, and going home at the end of the day carry more weight than any cost savings they may benefit from in an older, less life-safe building.

If the building doesn't pass your muster on life safety but works for your leasing interest, make the landlord upgrade the system as a condition to your leasing. Not after you move in (when the landlord will likely take forever to get around to it), but BEFORE you move in.

SECURITY

Security usually comes in the form of a guard who does little more than watch TV and eat sandwiches. Other buildings have a guard sit behind an impressive panel of lights, monitors and radios. But none of this is worth a nickel unless the guard is able to PERFORM a service for you. Keeping out the frequent door to door salesman is not security. Rushing to your suite when an irate visitor comes to your office, or escorting a terminated employee from the building is service. Also, keeping a log of visitors to the building is important when something is missing from your space. Remember, the security cost is in the building's operating expenses; you pay for it in your rent and will pay for the increase in its cost. So, in addition to confirming what the security routinely provides, make the landlord put into your lease those services they will provide without additional charge. Make it a condition to your lease. It is a small item for the landlord to agree to but huge to you if you need it.

Electronic security is fast becoming the norm in the age of industrial espionage and terrorism. Security devices which monitor every employee to enter or leave the space are available as are simple devices such as door buzzers and video recording. Considering the scope or expense of these devices, they may be installed as part of the tenant improvements.

EMERGENCY GENERATOR

Power outages are very common and while most companies take precautions to back up electronic information, it does little for getting out of the building when the electric goes out because of a storm or fire. Emergency generators generally operate emergency and life safety equipment, emergency lighting, and smoke removal systems. Some run the elevators at least to allow for lowering to the lobby to avoid any one becoming stuck in the elevator. Make sure your team has identified exactly what is powered by the generator and if you are a substantial user and a building that you are considering doesn't have one, require it as part of your negotiations. In some cases you may require one for your own personal business needs such as keeping an uplink communications system going, continue serving customers, telephones or computer systems. If you want to visit the 1890's in business, just try to operate yours with no computers or telephones. There is no better time to get someone else to pay for these items than when you are just looking and starting to negotiate.

6

OPERATING EXPENSES

Every manager's nightmare is the huge, unbudgeted, unanticipated invoice. Yet managers everywhere face the same problem—operating expense pass throughs. While rent continues
to be the most obvious financial aspect of any lease, there are
little known gremlins of economic surprise hidden behind rent.
On full service or gross leases, the quoted base rent per sq. ft. is
actually a combination of two forms of rent. The largest is the
capital portion from which the building owner pays the debt
service and generates profit. The remainder is the operating
expense portion which covers normal expenses associated with
the operation of a standard office building. These reflect such
fixed expenses as taxes and insurance and such variable
expenses as utilities, janitorial service, consumable supplies,
maintenance and repairs, etc.

In some markets or in certain buildings, different items such
as real estate taxes or utilities may be separated out in the lease
document for special handling or direct billing to the tenant (a
form of net lease). However for the purpose of ease, whether in
or separate from the operating expense language, the premise is
the same.

The operating expense portion of the rent rises as the cost of
services increases. This increase is passed through to the tenant
as additional rent. This is usually billed annually and the tenant

must immediately pay the lump sum increase PLUS be billed monthly for the anticipated increase for the upcoming year.

Most leases contain "STOP" provisions wherein the tenant begins to reimburse the landlord to pay for increases after the expenses exceed a specific number that is ordinarily determined under one of two structures, "Base Year" or "Base Amount". In either structure, a basis number is determined and above which the tenant is obligated to pay. The Base Year concept usually considers that the operating expenses as totaled in the first lease year of the tenant's occupancy becomes the base amount over which the landlord will charge the tenant. The Base Amount structure simply makes the declaration of the operating expense amount up front in the lease.

This is very good for the owner and investors who have pushed any increases off of their books and onto the tenant. These terms can also be just as negotiated by the tenant during the lease negotiations as any other lease term.

Would it not be absolutely wonderful for manufacturers, service providers, insurance companies and others to have the pre-established right that if it costs more to provide the service or product, you simply bill the client? The real estate owners are the one group which historically has enjoyed the privilege of knowing what they will spend and to avoid any deterioration of the return on investment, simply pass increases through to the tenants. If Boeing tried that on the U. S. Navy, it is doubtful that they would sell many jets. The owner does put up a plausible argument though, that these are consumable items by the tenant and therefore billable to the tenant, not carte blanche services in exchange for the rent. In deed, some of that argument holds water, but just because that argument holds water it does not mean you should shy away from the negotiations to improve your position. The tenant does have recourse, but only before the lease is signed as part of their leverage in negotiations; never after.

As an example to explain how the tenant gets billed for operating expenses, let's assume a full service rental of $20.00 per sq. ft. The operating expenses may be only $6.00 per sq. ft. which leaves $14.00 per sq. ft. for the owner to pay its debt and hopefully earn a return on its investment. After operating expenses reach $6.00 per sq. ft., the landlord's amount has stopped and the tenant starts paying any amount above it. Any amount above the $6.00 is the tenant's responsibility. The impact of these pass throughs can be significant. For example, an increase of just 50 cents per sq. ft. on a 10,000 sq. ft. lease will cost the tenant $25,000 over a five year lease term. 50 cents may only be 2.5% increase on the $20.00 per sq. ft. rent and viewed by some as rather insignificant, but how many more widgets or how much more service do you need to sell to your clients and customers to earn a net $25,000 to make up for an unanticipated $25,000 cost outlay? I hope this is starting to sink in. Can you imagine a pass through based on the increase in the cost of living of, say 5%? $50,000! Or worse, no cap or ceiling on how high the increase can go. And no motivation on the part of the Landlord to keep operating costs in line when they can just bill the tenants for any increases?

The "Base Year" structure of operating expenses is generally the safest to the tenant in that the base amount over which the tenant will be charged is based on actual operating expenses for either the previous calendar year or "Fiscal Year" of operations. Assuming the building has been operated ordinarily and with reasonable occupancy, the tenant will usually get billed the adjustment amount and the landlord's good faith projected estimate of the upcoming annual increase billed monthly in advance. Two caveats to this structure are 1) that the expenses are not increased due to the increased occupancy of the building, and 2) selecting the right Base Year is important when you are commencing a lease late in the calendar or "Base" year. This would allow the Landlord to bill you an increase much sooner. In these cases, a base year should be established as next year.

The Operating Expense "Base Amount" theory, sometimes knows as the "Expense Stop" is functionally different in that a specific expense is stated up front and at the time the expenses rise above that amount, the tenant gets billed. The caveats for this structure are both the increased occupancy of the building and that a real expense amount is used as a basis.

Building owners, forced to compete in the marketplace by showing a lower rental, may quote lower operating expense numbers than actual. By doing this, the landlord can hold their property up to the market looking as if the rent is lower than competitive buildings. Let's take our $20.00 per sq. ft. again, lower the "stop" to $4.75 and the owner can advertise space for $18.75 per sq. ft. without cutting his capital portion (where he makes his profit). The downside to the tenant will be that by using an artificially low base operating expense number and when the actual expenses are determined to be quite a bit higher, the tenant will be faced with an unbudgeted increase in rent. If the tenant fails to pay this increase, it could be put in default of the lease. Even if the default is cured, the default may have voided certain benefits the tenant may have had such as renewal or expansion options.

We were called upon to help a tenant who suffered just such a fate. Their 5,000 sq. ft. lease clearly stated $5.00 per sq. ft. for operating expenses as part of a $15.00 per sq. ft. full service rental rate. Remember, any increase above $5.00 per sq. ft. would simply be billed to the tenant. Barely one year after occupancy, whamo, the operating expense bill arrived stating the operating expenses had been determined to be $7.00 per sq. ft. A $2.00 per sq. ft. hit immediately or $10,000, and subsequent increases from this during the remainder of the lease were calculated to total over $20,000 to the tenant. In many circumstances, a landlord that knowingly misquotes the operating expense may be liable for misrepresentation, and in some cases, fraud. A worthwhile consideration, if you do suspect just such monkey business, is to contact all other tenants in the building, especially those that are larger and have more to lose. Without accusing the landlord of misrepresentation which could be libelous itself, simply indicate what has happened to you and seek to determine if something similar has occurred to them. Advise them what your intentions would be if it were proven that there was a problem (you would seek recourse by not paying the increase, put the Landlord in default and seek damages including the cost of performing such a review. Courts could also be sought for injunctive relief). A collective dispute from more than one tenant will have a profound effect on solving the problem.

A medium sized advertising and production firm leased 4,500 sq. ft. The rental had been negotiated successfully with the condition that the owner provided evidence that the operating expenses being quoted at the time of the lease were fair and accurate estimates of the actual costs. The landlord brushed over this giving general assurances that never would they treat a "good client" by overcharging. Eighteen months later, the "good client" tenant got a bill for $9,750. The land-lord knowingly misrepresented the operating expense base year amount of $4.75 per sq. ft. when in reality the actual operating expense amount was $6.25 per sq. ft. Balance due $1.50 per sq. ft. ($6,750) plus the estimated monthly amount of next years expense increase of $3,000. "DUE ON RECEIPT" Needless to say, this tenant flipped out, and justifiably so. Had the Tenant required the landlord warrant that the operating expenses of $4.75 per sq. ft. were fair and accurate, there would have been recourse.

One step further is to create a remedy for you if you find such abuses. A remedy can include offsetting rent or escrowing any disputed amount until resolved and without default to your lease. The provisions for doing this must be in the lease first. However, if it is not in the lease, escrowing the disputed amount in a bank with a receipt of its deposit to the landlord will usually suffice until the dispute can be resolved. Submitting it to a court as trustee until resolved can be persua-sive especially if the landlord did knowingly misquote rent. Language should be included in the lease to provide that the tenant may withhold paying a disputed amount or escrow an amount without being in default of the lease. One of the oldest tricks in the book is to send out large operating expenses and then follow up saying that non-payment of the expense will put the tenant in breech of the lease. Faced with fighting their landlord over an amount which may not be worth hiring an attorney to defend, many tenants simply acquiesce. As Winston Churchill said, "Never! Never! Never!". Never allow the landlord this ability on operating expenses or any other term of the lease.

Demand that the operating expenses of the building be pro-vided by having the landlord complete an operating Expense Breakdown form. During the building search period, the form is an excellent tool to smoke out possible abuses up front. Using the BOMA (Building Owners and Managers Association) or the Institute of Real Estate Management (IREM) Operating Expense books which monitor most all cities operating expenses, you, or your agent, can quickly and easily determine whether the quoted expenses are within reason.

Once a building is selected, the form should be attached to the lease as an Exhibit whereby the landlord warrants and represents that the stated amounts are fair and accurate.

Building not fully occupied.

Imagine also that a building is partially full, where the landlord is not paying for consumables associated with tenancy such as janitorial service, electrical or HVAC consumption, etc. In the event that the landlord is quoting you a full service rent (consisting of the capital and operating expense portions) based on the fact that the current operating expense in the quoted rent reflects the abnormal low occupancy of the building, you face a triple threat: 1) the ordinary increases in the cost of services and consumables, 2) the new cost of services and consumables as the building acquires more leases, and (Are you ready?) 3) your own new occupancy of the building will add to the services and consumables. Many leases account for this fuzzy circumstance by forcing the landlord to define the operating expenses as if the building is 90% occupied. This may seem like a solution, but I have been party to too many situations where the tenant got whipped after falling for (or not understanding) the relationship between occupancy and cost of services relative to a potential operating expense pass through. The lesson is simple: Avoid unscrupulous landlords or understand fully the risk of the increase in expenses, and plug it into your financial analysis. A year and a half after you move in when you are holding an unexpected bill for $12,250.18, you will have zero leverage if you did not address this initially.

While it is usually quite difficult to get a landlord to agree to no operating expense pass through, negotiate a reasonable percentage cap on the size of the increase and put it in the lease.

The lease must also contain language which allows the tenant to review the operating records of the building throughout the lease term, and for a period after the lease term should a dispute arise afterward. While this always felt good to have in the lease, it was somewhat of a red herring, however. Unless the amount is so financially substantive, there is little incentive to go through the hassle and expense. Secondly, few tenants have the understanding of what they would be looking at and whether an abuse was created or not. The landlord usually knows this and as a result usually agrees to such inspections. The landlord is very cleaver and subjective about what gets paid, and can defend almost anything when pressed. While it is not fair to say that every building owner uses less than truth in determining what operating expenses contain, it is fair to say that there exists a great freedom on behalf of the owner in determining what gets paid and what gets charged to the tenants.

Leases may contain general wording to define what operating expenses consist of while others will lay out a detailed laundry list of the specific elements which make up the operating expenses. Ordinarily, operating expenses also refer to elements relative to repairs and maintenance. It is usual that capital improvements are excluded from operating expense calculations. But frequently you will find the crafty landlord that considers the replacement of every square foot of carpet in the building, the redevelopment of the front entry and the improvements of other tenants to be expenses worthy of passing through to all of the tenants. A carefully worded definition of operating expenses excluding these types of things will keep the matter clean and avoid unnecessary surprises later. This is why short leases sometimes can be a liability to the tenant. If the lease has no such definition, then you have no way of knowing what you are looking at when you get your operating expense increase bill, and you have no manner to qualify the components that make up the bill.

Only a CPA or devoted property manager with daily experience in real estate operations can be of real value and the cost of providing such talent for what could be a several day job of reviewing the records is usually disincentive to do anything. Even if you could afford it, the reviewer might only simply codify the already incorrect information the landlord has told him. This provision ordinarily has no teeth. So, to give it teeth, add language that states the landlord must pay for at least one audit by a CPA or other entity selected by tenant during the lease and create provisions that offer recourse to the tenant to protect against unsubstantiated or unrealistic increases should they be discovered (such as offsetting rent, putting the landlord in Default).

For the most egregious and very expensive cases, and this can easily be the case if you are a large tenant, language should be included in the lease which provides that in the event the dispute can not be resolved by review or negotiation, then the tenant may seek injunctive relief by the courts from paying the disputed amount and continue the dispute either in court or through arbitration. Again, without putting the tenant in default of the Lease. Remember, there are few other areas in the life of leasing office space that can cause as much trouble as the operating expense pass through. Beware.

Excess Use and After Hours use—

Mandate that any excess usage and after hours costs by other tenants (especially the big users like CPA's) be calculated and removed from the building's operating expense overall calculation. However, if you think you may be a big user try to avoid this your self. Excess use is determined by kilowatt hours (kw/h). If billed, be sure there is a way to verify accurately what was used "premises-wide", not just a big computer. Some leases contain language which itemizes individual electrical items maximum kwh's. Determine a fixed basis kw/h premises-wide as the basis over which an excess use can be billed. Don't leave it vague, which then allows the landlord to make the determination after the fact and stick it to you. If you don't pay, you're in default (unless you have protected yourself against default with language in the lease). It makes no difference if you have a piece of equipment in the mail room which is by itself excessive kw/h if premises-wide your use is within or under the amount associated with your occupancy.

There are certain costs which usually are not to be calculated or included in the building operating expenses. The best example is parking garage operating costs. To the extent that such parking garage costs are paid by receipts collected by the building garage operator (another profit center) they must be removed from building operating expense cost.

Being knowledgeable and well represented is to everyone's advantage. landlords don't want angry, unhappy tenants anymore than tenants want unbudgeted surprises.

7

TENANT IMPROVEMENT ALLOWANCE

The single largest chunk of cash to the landlord in leasing office buildings is the financial contribution it must make in order to finish the space to the specifications of the tenant. A fairly simple principal of exchange of consideration: The tenant agrees to pay rent for years in exchange for the space having been built in such a manner that the tenant can appropriately occupy the space. The landlord almost always has determined what basic allowance of cash for the construction it will spend in exchange for the rent. Landlords develop this cash allowance in several ways and the two most common are 1) a financial proforma, established way back at the investment level and certain assumptions were made as to income, expenses, capitalization, etc. or 2) the numbers are made out of whole cloth (often based on what the market will bear or simply what the owner feels like). It is usually the bank or investors which see these proforma and the landlord attempts to keep within these limits or face answering tough questions from the bank or investors. Improving on these assumptions (e.g.: more rent and less cash out and less operating expenses) is the mission of every owner and good property management team.

Quantitative

How or why these proforma are developed (doors, lineal feet of drywall, etc.) are important to the LANDLORD (it had to determine what it was going to spend). The problem is that many Landlords rigidly apply these allowances and don't understand that it should simply be the total dollars. Who cares if the tenant is going to have gold leaf on the walls or six internal stair cases or more likely, have several more doors, more drywall, more outlets, etc. In some cases, the landlord will attempt to do an item-by-item comparison determining how much drywall is designed compared to their limit, or how many doors compared with their limit. This is an absolute waste of all professional's time. Big deal if you design 100 lineal feet of drywall more that the landlord wants to provide or use less doors than they expected to provide. Do not allow the landlord to impact your analysis of its building by their providing such a computation to you. Simply acknowledge the work accomplished and request your architect to provide a total construction cost estimate which will be compared to what the owner hoped to spend. (Even if it will be your goal to get the landlord to spend more than it expected.) Quick note: it is customary when touring properties for agents and landlords to get a feel for what kind of improvements you might require. Either say it has not been fully determined, or indicate the need for a great deal more than you need. If you have an open space plan requiring very little tenant improvements, keep that to your self as you need to negotiate for every dollar that the landlord would expect to have to pay.

Qualitative

Owners also spend way too much time concerning themselves with the quality standards of tenant finishes. When the original standards were selected, they ordinarily were simply chosen as the kind of finishes the basic building will provide like solid mahogany doors with brass hardware and 32 ounce cut pile carpet. Some landlords assume that this is static and cannot be beneath these standards of quality but neither can a tenant increase the quality of the items with out being responsible for the cost. They look at the quality of the finishes as a steel box out side of which the tenant can not go, at least not without penalty.

When I was working with a developer I was party to these limited and inane conversations and at the time couldn't understand why the tenant just stared at me. To make my point, I remember the guy from the facilities department of a large national firm telling me in his loud voice, "HOG WASH! IT'S ALL DOLLARS, STUPID." He got his way and I learned. In some cases, construction costs will be less than the amount the landlord expected to pay, which creates an opportunity in the negotiations to get the unused portion as cash, additional improvements or lower rent.

STANDARDS

There are certain buzz words that have been used with such proliferation in the real estate business that even those that use them have lost their meaning. More dangerous is when the same buzz word used by many different people is being used with different definitions. In tenant improvement lingo, the words "standard" and "standards" are tossed up at convenient times by landlords to indicate to you that you are about to blow through a red light at a train crossing. Having in their mind the quantities and quality of the finishes we reviewed above, you should be getting a sense that landlords like nice neat deals that don't wander to far from their concept of ideal. Each building has its predetermined ideal which is different from every other building. In many years, I have not seen two building's standard finish schedules that were alike. Upon hearing the word standard (which usually means your bumping up against a potential conversation for the landlord to defend it), courteously acknowledge the conversation, but ignore its value. Landlords negotiate everything and tenant improvement is no exception. In fact, for all the proforma the landlord has developed surrounding the construction costs, and despite their quoted "standard" construction allowance, this is a category that is usually always negotiated.

Remember, your goal is management of this process. Don't get muddled in techno-conversations on tenant finish allowance standards. You already have the Criteria/Needs Assessment complete, so you know what is needed. You have the Building Technical Breakdown complete and the Tenant Improvement Allowance breakdown form (in the Architectural Chapter) showing both what they are offering and what is already in the space (which might be of value or might need to be demolished) so you, your team and architect can accurately determine the financial viability or problems with a space.

Developing the hard construction costs is a process that will be developed in two stages: The Preliminary cost estimate and the Final construction estimate which is discussed later. This sounds like kindergarten, but there is a distinct difference. Remember, that to maintain control over the negotiations, you must have control over the information.

The preliminary cost estimate is determined within the walls of your team with the considerable input from your architect. As part of his or her job they must be able to have access to reasonably accurate construction cost prices preferably based on "unit pricing", as opposed to having to deliver full-blown construction drawings to a general contractor who takes two weeks to review them and discuss it with eleven subcontractors. You can not afford that sort of delay and nor can you afford the multiples of details, conversations and meetings required to deal with the actual sub-contractors who usually won't give an accurate bid unless the specifications are pinned down. This would be multiplied in difficulty if you have to go through this exercise at several buildings. You are not at that stage yet. You simply need to get a good, firm estimate of the expected construction cost which your team will compare with the building tenant improvement allowance.

Now you have enough information to accurately negotiate with the landlord as to the requirements they must meet in order to accommodate your Criteria. Remember, there is always room for negotiation. As part of your negotiations, don't request, indicate that these are the minimum requirements to meet your criteria. The cost may be beneath, above or at what the landlord wants to spend, which creates a framework for the landlord to respond to other issues, like rent, knowing what the out of pocket construction will be.

When negotiating the tenant improvement allowance, it is important to know what the landlord is using as a basis for construction. What portions of the common areas are to be built and expected to be paid for from your allowance? There are as many different ways of determining this as there are moods of the landlord, so your team must have this pinned down, which can easily be highlighted in the Tenant Improvement breakdown form. One easy way to get more cash for construction is to have the highest possible allowance number you can negotiate multiplied by the "rentable" area that will appear on your lease. You are not building the rentable, you're building the usable. If the load factor in the building is 14.5% you are getting 14.5% more cash to build your actual space. Obviously, if you're looking at buildings that do not charge on a rentable basis then this opportunity does not exist. However, you may be looking at several different buildings which have rentable and usable. Your architect will be able to calculate the available cash to build the area you will occupy.

During your negotiations on tenant improvement, the final cost may be above what the owner is willing to spend. Of course you can always pay the difference, which is exactly what the landlord wants you to do. What is better for you is for the landlord to pay for it and amortize the additional cost over the term of the lease which increases your occupancy cost. That is okay as long as you know how to handle it and compare against the other buildings you may be considering. Amortization is a great tool which means simply that you are borrowing the money from the landlord and paying it back with interest in equal monthly installments. Ordinarily, it is billed right into the monthly rent which means you only write one check. From a balance sheet point of view, this is terrific because it is paid as rent and ordinarily not considered as a long term loan. Had you gone to the bank and borrowed the same amount, it would show up on you balance sheet as a loan or long term liability. You can always go to the bank to borrow the money as an option, but by doing it through the landlord, it is likely you need not put up collateral or cut into your line of credit. Banks want collateral (unless you have a great relationship) and borrowing from the bank may create a lien on some property, personal or real estate or blanket lien.

The ideal obviously is to hold negotiations on this point until other elements have been agreed to, make it a condition of the lease, and have the landlord pay all the improvements as a concession.

When it costs less to build the space than the landlord is prepared to pay you have options also. First, keep this little secret from the landlord for now until you develop a plan. Remember the landlords want to spend as little money as possible and collect as much rent. Provided you are successful in attaining the rent you desire from the landlord (with the landlord assuming he is paying the allowance—remember the exchange of consideration) you should be able to 1) design, spend more of the landlord's money on luxuries like a full blown kitchen, terrific wall covering, glass partitions, marble top counters, whatever, 2) seek a proportionate reduction in the rent, 3) take the difference in cash, or 4) take the difference in rent abatement. The easiest and least noticeable is to design more. The landlord probably couldn't care less as long as his maximum isn't passed. In this case it may also be possible to "build" some of those items which would ordinarily be considered tenant's personal property like modular partitioning, computer cabling, telephone system or installation. These items can easily be provided through the general contractor or have your vendor become a sub-contractor to the general contractor. The downside is that for those items that are obviously used by the tenant and removable like desks, lamps, etc. the landlord takes a dim view of funding your property. If the underage is substantial, say $6.00 per sq. ft. on a 10,000 sq. ft., $60,000 would go along way, and it may be better to reduce the rent. But $3.00 per sq. ft or $30,000 is only equivalent to two months at a $20.00 per sq. ft. rent. Landlords usually have a problem in convincing themselves or their bank that they should turn over a check for the tenant's discretionary purposes, however aggressive developers that are rushing to pre-lease a building in order to make a financing deadline will eagerly pitch away cash to seal the deal.

When evaluating whether to pay for the improvements yourself, consider that, from an IRS point of view, any amount that has a "useful life" beyond a year ordinarily is to be depreciated over the term of its useful life. In the case of a lease, the IRS has provisions for three year, five year and longer periods for depreciation. That is to say, you ordinarily are prohibited from "expensing" the improvements, deducting the whole amount on your tax return in the year they occur. The IRS has some sticky little provisions regarding personal property and real property which, in the context of commercial office leasing, are frequently very gray. Simply have your accountant review the different situations with your team, make the appropriate calculation on the Financial Analysis form and the detail is covered.

FEES DUE REAL ESTATE BROKER

This chapter has been all about cash; managing or making the best use of landlord's cash. In real estate deals, everything is usually on the table for discussion and negotiation and I have seen landlords and developers negotiate on every possible economic component in a lease. The rent gets negotiated down, the Tenant Improvement Allowance gets negotiated up, free rent appears like magic, moving expense allowances are offered, parking costs are abated, and existing leases are taken over. Hell, I've seen cruises, cars and cash payments as inducements. It's all just cash. But time and time again, some arrogant landlords and developers declare the fee due the real estate agent is fixed in concrete or as holy a thing as if the shroud of Turin were draped around it. I've seen brokers make less on ten and fifteen year leases with larger tenants than they would have if they had made a much smaller five year lease. I've seen land-lords actually develop proposals where the financial gap in the negotiations between the tenant and landlord coincidently is an amount similar to the real estate brokerage fee; leaving the poor broker to act as if all this is her fault; or that the tenant will have to increase rent to pay for the fee. Hog wash again. Having a pistol-packing office tenant rep professional by your side for three, six, twelve or eighteen months is wise. These professionals only get paid by what deals they represent, no dif-ferently than an insurance agent, they eat what they kill. In some markets where real estate commissions vary wildly, it makes sense that this fee be at least roughly estimated or fixed to assure parity from building to building. As the tenant, you have every right to make this demand of the deal economics, and to assure your team members are appropriately and ade-quately compensated for the experience, skill and professional-ism they provide you. If the landlord is either too cheap to pay the appropriate fee, or too arrogant, then walk away. If the landlord is shaving cash so close, you probably should consider his financial stability at some risk. And if the landlord is hesi-tant out of principle or spite, you don't want him as a landlord. Use a good strong tenant representation agreement with your agent, establish the fee, have this agreement submitted to the landlord and agreed to (AND attached to the lease as an Exhibit to protect your agent), or walk away. There is a new world: The tenant, the cash provider for the landlord, is the engine. The tenant has all the leverage. There is a real joy in simply telling the landlord to go away. If he really wants you as a tenant, he will come back and agree.

8

ARCHITECTURAL DESIGN AND SPACE PLANNING

A good many architects provided to a tenant by the landlord are usually good vendors of the landlord. That is, the landlord relies upon them to expeditiously turn around plans and manage the process. It is also the job of the Landlord's architect to work in a manner (a mind set) that will design the office space with the most conservative use of the landlord's money for construction. With this predisposed mind-set of the architect to not spend his or her client's money, the complete effort is not given.

In a meeting with a good developer client, an architect friend of mine who was explaining to the tenant how he could gain by adding a kitchen (and a few other "non-standard" items) was literally kicked in the shin under the table by the developer/landlord to stop bringing up things which were going to increase the cost of the construction. When traditionally the architect depends on his or her livelihood from the good paying commercial real estate developers and landlords, the architect has little other choice than to do as told and simply provide the basics, no frills, and in many cases no efficiency.

This leaves the tenant to either accept the space as drafted or, worse, not know any better.

When considering several buildings, you must have completed a Tenant Improvement Breakdown. There are two concepts at play simultaneously which need to be defined in order to avoid confusion and gain a true understanding of dollars. It is this confusion and lack of understanding the landlord is banking on so as to avoid any additional outlay of cash. But you must be informed in order to make available those elements for the construction of your office which go directly to solving your problems and satisfying the criteria and needs you established at the outset. It will be essential to understand what the existing conditions are at each building; what value is already in the building BEFORE construction. It will different for every building. In those cases where the space has already been previously occupied by a tenant, your architect will be able to determine what residual value is in the improvements (Doors, Frames, HVAC, Grid, Lights, etc) and what is non-valuable and which must have cash to replace or add (carpet, walls that need to be removed, electrical wiring, etc.).

From a marketing point of view, there may be confusion while you are considering several buildings when the different buildings are quoting different Tenant Improvement Allowance amounts. Here is an example why you need to ignore all these elements until the architect has determined the existing conditions, and the planned use of dollars. Two new office buildings on the market at the same time were offering very similar dollar amounts per sq. ft. for rent. However, one building was advertising a substantially higher Tenant Improvement Allowance. At first glance, it appeared to be a handsome draw to the uninformed, and for some tenants, they got caught in the hype. The reality was that the higher advertised amount was necessary just to bring some of the basic systems in place, like major duct-runs, sprinkler head distribution, etc. The reality was that by comparison, the building that had quoted the lower Tenant Improvement Allowance actually was providing greater direct dollars to the tenants because most major systems, ceiling grid, sprinklers, etc had already been installed in the building shell construction cost.

A Tenant Improvement Allowance declared by any building is, on its face, irrelevant unless it is viewed in relationship to the present conditions of the building, and the need you have for construction. The Tenant Improvement Allowance form must contain the value of the existing conditions in one column and the value of the TIA in the other. Most landlords have this information completed as part of their proforma and your architect can easily complete it. This being done for each building you are considering will smoke out the real dollar amount you will have available.

The configuration of the building and the floor plan may have a considerable impact on the efficiency of your office design. Items of consideration include the depth of space from the interior corridor (or core) to the outside wall. Shorter distances provide less flexibility in designing exterior offices and interior uses simultaneously. Whereas with greater distances, the office design can accommodate exterior offices, interior offices with a sizable work area in between. These larger distances work well for most larger office users that can double stack offices and work area. Some older buildings were built in shapes that conformed to given land sizes and the developer spent more time thinking about how to get the project off the ground and less on how the space would lay for tenants. Because of this lack of concentration, some buildings are handicapped with very narrow width dimensions between the core and the windows. This has a considerably negative impact to larger tenants who find they must lease more space than anticipated simply to have all their required improvements.

While not as critical as the core-to-window dimension, the distance between the window mullions can impact the design of the offices along the window line. Typically, and as good construction practice the walls built between private offices or other rooms that are on window lines should be built to abut the window mullion rather than against the glass line. A building with 4 feet between mullions can accommodate room dimensions at 4 foot intervals, such as 8'xlO' or 12'xlO' or 16'xlO. The *width* becomes the fixed dimension and the *depth* becomes the variable. This example holds true for mullions at 5 foot intervals. Some buildings have been built with varying mullion dimensions, such as 5 feet then 4 feet then 5 feet then 3 feet, etc. This makes the design more tricky and the end product more dubious as one office may have a three foot window and a five foot window with a mullion that divides the two in a position that makes the room look awkward. The input from your architect is very helpful here to figure what works for your firm's use. For the price of office space, one should not be compelled to accept awkward offices.

The public access to an office space is often forgotten or at least left to the building owner to determine. The width of such public corridors varies from 3 to 6 feet depending on the age or design of the building or the indifference of the owner. It is peculiar to walk down a narrow corridor where no two persons can walk abreast. Generally, a wider corridor that is designed well can be considered an extension of the image of the office space.

Rentable-to-Usable Ratio. The measurement of office space and the buzz words associated with it can be confusing. It can also lead to very expensive conditions. Real estate brokers may use similar terms as building developers but the two may be different enough to cause design difficulty and possibly rental increases. The Building Owners and Managers Association (BOMA) has established a well recognized and accepted definition and form of measuring office space (see Chapter 5). This has been extremely helpful. A story going around when I was fresh in the business was that a tenant, confused about how the office space was measured, asked the developer what points of measurement were used to come up with the tenant's square footage. The developer nodded and proceeded to point to the interior wall near the corridor as one dimension and pointed to the yellow line in the middle of the street outside as the other. I cannot say that this is a true story, however I can say that I have been involved in numerous discussions about the validity of the measurement of space that this story has been used to drive home my point.

In addition to the pure measurement needs of an architect and to determine the amount of space upon which to multiply the rental rate, the differences between a number of buildings in how they calculate their measurements will considerably impact your financial analysis. Affordable Lease Analysis software is also readily available through the internet. Your agent should already have this ability, but retail financial analysis software is now so affordable and intuitive, you might want to have control of it yourself.

The higher the Loss (or load) factor, the less efficient the space shall be for the purposes of calculating rent. The usable area is the definitive area that the tenant will occupy. Grossing up this usable area to include the tenants proportionate share of the building's common areas will increase the final figure on which the rental is multiplied. But all is not as it appears. A major stock brokerage firm had plans of leasing office space in one of two buildings. Building number one, a brand new granite and glass beauty had a rental rate of $22.00 per sq. ft. and building number two, an older dowdy building had a rate of $18.00 per sq, ft., both full service leases. Their attention was naturally directed toward the lower priced building number two. However, the higher priced, new building had a rentable-to-usable ratio of 10.7%. The old dowdy had a ratio of 18.5%. Additionally, building two had air-conditioning/heating units within the space surrounding the interior of the exterior wall. The depth of this unit was three feet which meant the tenant's real use was three feet inside the point from which the space was measured. Taking into account the higher load factor and the unusable area, the older dowdy building actually cost this firm more than if they had leased the new beauty. This firm could have had a silk purse, instead it chose a sow's ear. Interestingly, this firm is no longer in business. The point is: Don't listen to the landlord or the marketing material or the silver tongue listing agent. Let your team smoke this entire element out.

9

GOVERNMENTAL ISSUES

In office leasing, we usually consider the physical and financial elements that are obvious to us. Rent, free rent, tenant improvement allowance, building design and the other details take a large portion of our mental space and time, however make room for more. When Donald Trump sails into town to consider building a new casino or hotel, or when a large manufacturing firm sniffs around a city, the newspapers and news programs are full of stories how the mayor rolled out the red carpet, the aldermen pressed flesh, the governor offered a proclamation and union representatives grinned ear to ear. Why? It's economic development. Whether it is a jumbo jet manufacturer or brassiere manufacturer, economic development of the cities, counties and states is so aggressive to take on Herculean proportions. Big companies mean big jobs, big construction, big wages, big taxes to pay for new fire trucks, new roads; it's the American capitalist experiment in microcosm.

But you do not have to be General Motors to receive attention. Yes, the large companies are trophies to some cities, but the smaller companies, millions and millions of them run the engine consistently, day in and day out. Because of many companies relative obscurity as compared to large corporations, so too do the economic development groups tend to overlook them. However, with some effort, you can get them to notice you and find gold. For whatever reason, manufacturing firms more so than others seem to get the attention of economic developers. But not-so-large firms do also. Take a small widget manufacturer employing 46 people that can no longer use its 100 year old building in an urban area and wishes to relocate to a single level, new building with room for growth. Remember, it is the job of economic development groups to develop economic growth, large and small. With a little prodding, but not as much fanfare, the economic developers will wine and dine, show slide shows indicating the values and benefits of certain communities, make introductions to other companies that have already made the move, introduce banks that are ready and willing to lend, suppliers who are willing to supply and customers who are ready to buy; all just for the asking. These groups do a wonderful job in convincing legislators to reduce or abate real estate taxes as an incentive to build in order to get the brass ring of the employees working and spending their paychecks in their community. They are the gateway to low interest loans, grants for new technology or tax deductions for each new employee hired. There are so many different possible goodies economic developers can provide or influence that it can be like Christmas morning.

Okay, good for manufacturers, but you're an office user, insurance, book sales, professional head hunter, advertising, franchiser, or the executive/administrative office for a manufacturer in another city. The opportunities of economic development incentives also apply to you. But you have to go after them as opposed to them finding you. Contact the economic development department in your county, city and state and have them explain the different possibilities. Some cities may have very positive elements while others may have negatives like a stiff employee earnings tax or higher than normal business taxes. Although you are an office user, there are state and federal dollars available for job growth in service industries. These all need to be laid out for comparison. When the real estate market is very difficult for the tenant and finding good alternative sites to create options for your self is tuff, these economic development agencies can be just the leverage you need to either ferret out unknown opportunities of office space or even just create the added leverage you need to better your position at another location. Your employees represent high paid salaries (usually much better than manufacturing): very prime prizes for any economic development group.

A large firm really wanted to remain in their present building but the rent being offered by the landlord was much higher than normal because of the tight market. Moving was not of interest because of the cost and the proximity to several big clients. Moving to the county was quite possible but not of real interest. When they thought the negotiations would produce no more fruit with the building owner (the landlord knew there was no other spot in downtown for them to go), the tenant was introduced to the economic development team for a fast-growing, wealthy suburban community with plenty of office space and plenty of land on which to build a building. After having been informed of every possible economic enticement and meeting the mayor, the economic development team met the tenant as a piece of land worthy of developing. Word was quickly disseminated of the tenant's strong interest and it was made sure that the owner of the downtown building was particularly aware. Within several days, faced with the "reality" that the tenant had good, viable options and was poised to move, the downtown building's negotiations quickly improved to a point where a deal was set. Not really mischief, but another important reminder to always have options and choices for use as real alternatives or just negotiating strength.

If you do end up using the benefits of an economic development program, they are also excellent motivation builders for your employees when they hold open houses at your new office and rain praise on your company.

And do not discount the value of your present city or county from where you may move. Once aware that you may be leaving, (and if they don't, then tell them) your own community usually will take notice, rally the troops and develop a package of incentives to keep you. Better late than never.

10

THE LEASE

The lease document so frequently is perceived as the behemoth, insensitive beast that after being signed gets sent to lease heaven hopefully never to be seen again. Lawyers parse words and froth over nuance wording as if to protect against the most catastrophic circumstances. Owners repulse at the very thought of their precious language (that they paid thousands of dollars to prepare) being picked apart. In fact, most landlords using either basic leases with skeletal information or leases containing 40 pages of terms and 11 pages of riders which can be used as doorstops, frequently indicate that there can be no changes. The poor tenant sits on the side lines, waving as if to say "remember me, I'm paying the bill!" The reality is, not only can you modify nearly every term in the lease, but if you really want, like some large national tenants do, you can provide your own lease. The lease should not be viewed as the anti-Christ at all. On the contrary, a good, ugly, carefully put together lease will save you years of problems, disputes, court appearances and money. While a sale contract is designed to govern the activities of the parties prior to and up to a closing, a lease governs the activities of the parties for years and decades. Drafted badly or even slightly wrong, and many are, it can be indentured servitude. The key to making the lease work well is to make it come alive with provisions which work well in a multitude of circumstances, which fairly well address most difficulties that may arise over its life; and to make it readable and well understood. The problem with many leases is that there has been little working knowledge of the hand-in-hand relationship between ownership and management, management and leasing, services and tenant's needs. The lease just becomes flat words crammed into little paragraphs no one really cares ever to read unless they're preparing a law suit.

While the lease usually deals with the default of the tenant in any minor event, most landlord default provisions are limited to major financial default. Evaluate the stability or viability of the landlord as part of your work. For years the paradigm was to treat the tenant on the same financial scale as a consumer, determining credit worthiness, running D&B's, checking on the personal financial situation of the tenant, even hand wringing over the nature of the business of the tenant. While the landlord is certainly due some comfort of your ability to meet your rent, if there is one thing the last decade has taught us is that the landlord must also be scrutinized as to its financial viability and management style. Talk with other tenants in the building. If the landlord loses the building to foreclosure or the ownership, in whatever form, files for bankruptcy, your hard fought-for rights could go up in smoke. Never mind the grass not getting cut, how about having your lease terms invalidated with no recourse. The landlord boiler plate lease invariably contains two good clauses for them: "Tenant's Default", and "Landlord's Remedies to Tenant's Default". Oh they're great, you step out of line for a second and you'll be grabbed by the back of the neck like a school yard bully. But rarely do these leases contain provision for the Landlord's Default or Remedies to the Tenant for the Landlord's Default. Even a noted legal eagle who wrote a book for almost every clause to be put into an office lease failed to even mention the prospect of landlord default. The court house (and the court house steps) are full of cases where the landlord got into trouble. While it is likely that a new owner will step in or a bank or court will appoint a trustee, and the light bill will be paid and the grass cut, but what about your renewal option, what about the $40,000 security deposit, what about the commitment the landlord gave you that you could have 15 reserved parking spaces or the expansion area or what about the cancellation clause you successfully negotiated and need in order to move to Texas. That will make you wake up at 3:00AM. For landlord default provisions, the simplest manner is to convert all the preexisting tenant default language to being mutual for the landlord.

Here are a few other examples. Most boiler plate leases contain provisions such as the tenant irrevocably authorizes the landlord to execute and deliver in the name of the tenant any subordination if tenant fails to do so. This usually occurs when a building changes hands (and many times because the owner lost the building to the lender) or refinancing occurs. To agree at the lease execution that you will be forced to indicate your subordination four years hence is absurd without the assurance that you enjoy all the terms of the lease and are assured of quiet enjoyment and non-disturbance.

When a landlord defaults, it may manifest itself in the obvious lack of service to the tenant. If the landlord defaults and fails to perform any of their obligations under the lease, the tenant, at its option, should be able to perform the landlord's obligation or cause performance of landlord's obligation and deduct the reasonable cost thereof from the rent. A simple self-help clause like this can keep the tenant in control when the landlord has lost his. Most leases are one-way defaulters—the tenant, leaving silent, or very few, the provisions for landlord default. When buildings change hands, landlords go away, buildings get taken by the bank, or they file for bankruptcy, be sure your lease contains strong enough clauses to protect your lease provisions.

Also on tenant default, many leases contain a nasty little provision that the tenant is in default if it files for bankruptcy or is filed against for involuntary bankruptcy. Gee, that's nice. Three creditors gang up on the tenant, file for involuntary bankruptcy and the tenant is now in default of the lease and must cure the default or the landlord can force you out. I don't think so. Ask your attorney to adjust the lease to reflect default only in the event the tenant is "adjudicated" bankrupt.

Another example is the time amount to cure a default. Many leases contain fuses so short to cure a default, economic or non-economic, that you'll be in material breech before you have a chance to get the lease out of the storage room.

Expansion

Frequently considered as more of a stepchild to the terms negotiated for the premises you seek to lease, expansion opportunities should be considered as one of those key terms that jumps to join his real brothers and sisters at the beginning of the negotiations and carefully crafted in the lease document. Working from the standpoint of your needs assessment and criteria and your view into the future of your business, only you can understand what circumstances you expect to occur, and what goals you have for your business. Dividing up your company into parts which you can more definitively get a feel for, consider each element as its own line of business with its own growth or contraction needs. One would assume that if it is your interest to generate greater and larger sales over the next three, five or ten years, consider constructing how you will achieve this in relationship to how these functions will be housed. Increasing sales ten percent per year means what? Can this ten percent increase the performed by your existing staff? How many people will be required to expand your core business? How many people will be required to expand to new customers or to push into new lines of business? Accordingly, as this requirement for additional square footage grows to accommodate more employees, so too does this affect other areas. Does your goal of increasing sales increase customer service or administrative functions? Does your marketing group need to generate those new sales?

While the architect can reasonably develop compatible adjacencies of all your business functions such as sales, administration, marketing, human resources, operations, and finance you have to give him or her the directions to understand this growth and relationship.

The initial square footage you see in the real estate market therefore is really only the first stage of many in your growth plan. Cementing oneself into a fixed or finite box of square footage with the knowledge of your anticipated growth is fine if that square footage can, in fact, accommodate your growth in it. That is programming. Where the limits get reached and burden develops is where expansion thinking should become a plan. If this happens you must then consider the burden to you financially and otherwise of not growing.

Lesser sized tenants finding themselves between several larger tenants know well the pressure of the likelihood at their lease expiration that they will be required to relocate in order to accommodate the other tenants. Having no option but to move out or relocate within the building will have a high financial impact on your profit and loss when you are forced to capitalize the cost of a relocation you really didn't necessarily want. So, for the sake of preventing unnecessary future costs, good expansion right provisions will do just that. Bringing expansion onto page one of your financial requirements also provides the landlord with the knowledge of your expected growth and stability.

Conversely, day one in landlord school has taught landlords that expansion options can be a pain to manage. Many landlords find it difficult to manage the varying expansion rights of different tenants and the requirement to provide notices to tenants of the availability of space. Occasionally a tenant will forget the date of their expansion option also.

Securing additional area compatible with your programming can take a few forms: 1) hope there is square footage or 2) know there will be square footage when and if you need it. Formalizing expansion into rights can take a few forms: 1) An outright agreement to take a certain square footage on a certain date, 2) A Right of First Refusal, and 3) a Right of First Offer.

A Right of First Refusal establishes a process whereby the landlord will first have consummated the lease terms with another tenant, but before he signs the lease, you have the right to refuse that lease and then lease it yourself under the terms the landlord negotiated with the other tenant. You in essence have no bargain in the deal, just take it or leave it. Some ROFR's also state the fixed terms the expanding tenant will enjoy, thereby forcing the landlord to seek other tenants at their negotiated terms while knowing about the existing terms.

A Right of First Offer turns that around in that upon the availability of certain space, the landlord must give you the first right to lease it before offering it to other tenants or the open market. In this case, terms can be negotiated as part of your lease to establish some financial parameters of the terms of the expansion area. Landlords hate accepting what terms they will accept in three or five years into the future, but with the leverage of your interest in the building most tenants can achieve some limitations on terms rather than accepting expansion at unknown terms.

You may also consider any multiple of these expansion rights. For example, you can secure a fixed option to lease the adjacent 2,000 square feet at the 30th month of the lease, have a Right of First Offer on another area, and a Right of First Refusal on yet another. Thought out carefully, these can be adjacent or elsewhere in the building.

Forget the monkey on the back of the landlord (which he or his agent or property management will surely verbalize). Forge ahead and pin these down.

While expanding any new area into your existing lease will dove-tail all the lease terms into it, several terms particular to the expansion spaces must be tailored, such as what form of rent will be charged, what the condition of the expansion area will be and what the tenant improvement allowance will be from the landlord necessary to make the new area compatible to your use and design. An expansion area that is unusable to you without the landlord's contributing money to modify the space only guarantees you the expense. If the space were to remain unoccupied, then a complete Tenant Improvement Allowance such as you negotiate for the initial area, plus increases for time, is appropriate. If the expansion area is completely unusable to you in that format, then additional cost must be negotiated to demolish the existing improvements. Rent should be negotiated on each of these expansion alternatives also. The best being that you have predetermined the exact rent, the opposite being at a fuzzy market rent. If you are going to expand into a 10,000 square foot area at a market rent determined only by holding a finger up to the wind when the landlord is actively leasing space in the building with competitive leasing terms, such as free rent, why should you not benefit from these things just because you are the landlord's bird in the hand.

Contraction

On the contrary, if you know that by technology, for example, you will likely require less employees in an area, or you have an expectation that a portion of your company will relocate, negotiate into the lease the provision which will allow you to turn back to the landlord certain square footage. While landlords are particularly un-fond of this sort of thing, using your Columbo-style of "just one more thing" and indicating to the landlord that with this agreed to, a lease can be signed, you will likely be successful, even if you have to go up the decision stream to get it.

Rent Increases

Lease documents frequently contain provisions for rental adjustments. Even if you have an understanding that the rental is quoted at a certain per square foot amount, without clarity on the rental in each year, you may be dealing with imprecise language. These increases usually take the form of some multiplier such as an annual increase in the Consumer Price Index or other index specific to the area the building is located in. It must be determined first exactly what is expected to be multiplied and therefore increased. Remember that in full service leases, the rent is a combination of the Capital Portion and the Operating Expense Portion. Many leases have separate clauses for the handling of increases in operating expenses which we addressed earlier in this book in the Operating Expense Chapter. If it is reasonable to assume the tenant must be responsible for the increases in operating expenses, then it would be an exponential mistake to accept that simultaneously the base rent (consisting of the capital portion and expense potion) be as well multiplied by some multiplier. It would be precise that if there is an agreement to adjustment in the rent, that it be clearly understood what is increasing: the capital portion, the operating expenses or both. In heavily landlord oriented markets, a take it or leave it situation may result where the tenant has little choice. But even in this environment, to avoid conflict and misunderstanding in the future, be sure each category is clearly understood as to how each is being treated for increase. Limiting any rental increase in these categories is based on the market conditions no differently than other terms in the lease. While it may be desired to have zero rent adjustments over five years, it may be reasonable to understand that operating expenses, like the cost of living, do increase. It may be unreasonable, considering the market, to also increase the capital portion. Your situation can only be determined by your market and the leverage you have at each building. At one building you may have success in placing various limitations of increases while at others you will be unsuccessful. In any event, simply account for what you have negotiated and enter any good faith expectations or defined increases in the lease analysis software to put each building on an apples-to-apples basis.

Subleasing and Assignment

Subleasing is usually dealt with by either indicating the absolute refusal to permit subleasing without certain financial stability provisions of the subtenant being met, or a general agreement to subleasing with the landlord's consent. Subleasing may not be high on your radar when you are considering new office space now, but in seven years when you need to move to another city, downsize or relocate to another building to accommodate your growth, a flexible and tenant friendly subleasing provision is worth gold. Consent from the landlord should at least be not unreasonably withheld. Most state's statutes provide that this is the case by law, but there are many states that still permit landlords to be capricious, intractable and arbitrary. Modifying the subleasing clause is a throw away for the landlord because you maintain financial responsibility for the rent and the lease terms. Assignment, on the other hand, where the financial responsibility shifts entirely away from you, usually will have with it the specific requirement of financial stability in order to garner the landlord's agreement. Agreement on both provisions then gives you complete control to mitigate your losses in the event that you must continue with one leasing obligation while commencing another elsewhere.

Rent Abatement—IRS Section 467

While negotiation for free rent as an inducement is somewhat routine in office leases, there are some occasions where large amounts of free rent are viewed as a large cash transaction by the Internal Revenue Service. A little known, but influential IRS provision, Section 467, can result in a building owner having to report rental income earlier than actually collected and the tenant may have to report the same amount as rent expense earlier than actually paid. Section 467, although originally intended as a tax avoidance reform provision, may translate into far reaching adverse economic effects between landlords and tenants if the matter is not first fully defined. Section 467 is important because of its impact on routine commercial leases where it can be applied in ways to actually modify the intent that the parties had agreed regarding the timing of rental payments. If a lease is tested to be subject to 467 provisions, any rent concession or free rent period although not received by the landlord will have to be reported as received. The tenant too would be forced to modify the rent schedule. While this section is of real danger to the landlord as the penalty to fail to report 467 rental payments correctly may cost excessive damages, the tenant can be drawn in defacto because of the failure to report. The specific details that define "467 Rental Agreements" are complex and confusing. And stating in the lease that the lease is not subject to Section 467 is not sufficient if on its face it would meet the test. Competent legal and tax advice should be consulted as to the application of this section to any large rental concession situation.

Remember to hire a strong, tenant-oriented, good, poker-playing attorney. He or she will likely be the one to enforce these provisions against the landlord when the time comes.

11

LEASE MONITORING AND LEASE SUMMARIES

Lease Synopsis

As soon as the lease is executed, it is important not to just put the lease away and forget about it. The lease will contain several key elements which need to be kept in front of you for action and in some cases, preparation before an action. The simplest way to start this is to re-cook each of the salient elements into plain English. Restate the legal mumbo jumbo and craft a few sentences which best summarize the important points of the topic. Be sure to show the certain lease clause and paragraph number in order that when you need to refer to the legal language, you won't have to pore over all the language, but simply go right to it. This is particularly important for the future, for when there will be some one else handling the office lease or a problem requiring attention.

Critical dates

Your lease will contain dates which require you or the landlord or anybody associated with your occupancy to take an action. Highlight the date and pull it aside with a brief explanation. Just like the synopsis, describe in brief what the date is about and pull the Article and paragraph number in order to refer to the lease in the accurate spot. There are also dates that may benefit you if someone doesn't take an action which you also need to monitor. Lease documents get long with exhibits, addenda and riders, so be exact where the governing language is. If there is associated language in another part of the lease, highlight it and explain. Some dates indicate that by a date if you DON'T act you loose; like renewal options that automatically kick in if you fail to give notice, or your expansion opportunity is gone because you simply didn't write a one sentence letter.

Consider strongly also capturing the critical dates of all other tenants that may effect your occupancy and growth. There may be dates he has to live by also. Many a landlord has negotiated expansion rights which very rarely get triggered because the date came and went without action. Get as many dates as possible. Capture their expansion option dates, right of first refusal dates, right of first offer dates, renewal option notice dates and others so you know when they have to notify the landlord, or better, they forgot and now your ability to expand has just become superior to their lost rights. If any specific date requires work or time prior to its date, such as it may take three months evaluation to decide whether to execute your expansion option, be sure to create another critical date sufficiently early to deal with the date you must act. Remember knowledge is power and you are just setting the stage for the next negotiation with the landlord with your leverage in place.

Lease Alerts

Have every critical date entered into your personal and corporate electronic scheduler; any place that will always automatically appear when required. These dates do you no good stuffed in a file some place that will likely be forgotten, they must be kept alive. And when they do pop up, take them seriously by delegating them to someone who will investigate the details and provide you with options on how to deal with them.

A FEW CLOSING
COMMENTS

It will be many years before you have to undertake such a project again, and in some cases you may never, either by default or design. The message I have attempted to deliver to you is mastery and control over all elements, rendering you never to be subordinate or reactive to the elements, as so often is the case in office leasing and in real estate. Your employees will be affected by this, even your spouse will notice possible stress as you undertake an office relocation or renewal. I am hoping that these tips will enable you to avoid all stress relative to this undertaking. If you do become stressed out, read this book again or the relative section. State to your team members the same thing and give them a copy of this book to keep handy.

Also, don't negotiate all things at once. Plan which items you should stage along the line. Office leases are substantial financial instruments, even if you are a smaller tenant. Don't spill your jellybeans in the lobby. If you know that you will be seeking a large concession from the landlord or asking for his acceptance of a particularly thorny element, then negotiate to agreement on some items and hold back others until the landlord has sufficiently invested the amount of time, energy and money to think you are nearly at the alter. Do this with your present landlord as well if you intend to renew, but don't let him think you intend to remain. If you need some time or more leverage to keep the landlord on the hook, nothing gets a landlord quite so pregnant like asking him for a large photograph, rendering of the building or an aerial photo to share with employees and customers. Or, ask the landlord for a draft lease document for initial review. Whether you are sincere or not about your real intent, this type of request produces endorphins and serotonin in all landlords.

Turn the negotiations around. Instead of submitting an RFP (Request for Proposal) to the landlord, to whom you would then be reactive in the negotiation, submit an Offer to Lease proposal of your own in the form of a Summary of Salient Terms. A letter of intent, while not binding, certainly creates the stage that you intend to do something. But you may not. You may be just negotiating for better terms with one landlord, or at another building altogether, or even to re-lease where you are.

Use the media if you need to. It hurts no one if the paper "discovers" you are considering the county location, when it is the terms with the city location you are actually seeking to improve.

Above all, enjoy this process, because it is multi-faceted and brings a large pool of personalities and talented people into the scene. And, let's be honest. No one ever died from leasing office space. But everyone that does is participating in the great industrial, capitalist machine: to be better, healthier, wealthier and wiser more so tomorrow than today.

Feel free to contact me at chrisdesloge@aol.com

END

BIOGRAPHY

Christopher D. Desloge spent twenty years in the commercial real estate field. He has served as Leasing Manager for numerous metropolitan office towers and suburban office buildings in St. Louis, Missouri. In these capacities his responsibilities included all leasing activity coordinated with property management, construction, marketing and legal review.

With the in-depth experience of real estate development and leasing from working with respected Landlords, he developed two firms exclusively representing office tenants.

Desloge has been a member of the Society of Industrial and Office Realtors (SIOR); he has addressed the Building Owners and Managers Association (BOMA) as keynote speaker on Tenant Representation. His Tenant Representation firm was highlighted as unique small business in St. Louis, Missouri's Regional Commerce & Growth Association's <u>Commerce Magazine</u> and as a noted specialist in the field, published numerous articles for the <u>St. Louis Business Journal</u> as a contributing editor.

Desloge has served as an arbitration judge serving the Council of Better Business Bureaus, was a founding member and member of the Board of Directors of the International Tenant Representative Alliance (ITRA) and sits on several boards of directors of not for profit organizations. His reputation and skill have earned him the respect and representation of such noted companies as Xerox, Charles Schwab, Ohio Casualty Insurance, Hanover Insurance, Commercial Union Life, Medicine Shoppe International, Kelly Services, numerous law and accounting partnerships and many not for profit organizations. He has represented companies of all sizes, bringing the leverage as a large transaction specialist to all tenants enabling each to succeed counter to the landlord's control and influence in commercial real estate transactions.

NOTES

NOTES

0-595-31166-0